Three Thoughts Couple Devotional:

Engaging the Power of Our Minds and Hearts to Cultivate a Lifestyle of Intimacy

Alex A. Avila

Three Thoughts
Couple Devotional

Engaging the Power of Our Minds and
Hearts to Cultivate a Lifestyle of Intimacy

Alex A. Avila

All Scriptures quoted from *New International Version (NIV)* Bible.

Library of Congress Control Number: 2017912891

ISBN-13: 978-0999257500

ISBN-10: 0999257501

DEDICATION

To my lovely Claudia.

Because of our Father, friendship and faith, our best days are ahead.

"A cord of three strands is not easily broken."

Ecclesiastes 4:12

Contents

PREFACE

Why Three Thoughts? Well, our minds are creative, innovative and unique. Our values, beliefs and life-guiding principles are shaped, reinforced and repeated by our life experiences. Our experiences help us create memories, which further reinforce our future thoughts, words and actions. Therefore, our thoughts have tremendous power! How we think about our partner and relationship each day shapes the quality of our connection.

It seems that most people today are very busy. How do you stay on track and not give in to what competes for your attention? Distraction is an enemy of connection. So, what helps you stay focused on your partner and relationship? Classes, retreats, conferences or small groups? Would you have time to read another book?

Personally, I fit into a classification of humans that do not finish everything they start. I do not ready every page on every book I begin reading. I don't complete every project I take on (even with realistic optimism). If you have trouble believing this, just ask my wife! My list of unfinished projects still lingers at dangerous levels. So, would I be consistent starting a new activity that I can promise to do every single day (even one that I believe will considerably help me)? Are you kidding me? The answer is no. But, when I have made a real commitment—one that includes a thoughtful, realistic plan to overcome unexpected barriers—I can be successful. That is, when I want it bad enough.

So, I can identify with the difficulties in remaining focused and consistent. I know that forgetting a day here or there is a high likelihood for some people. Getting off track seems too easy after a few misses. But, I didn't want readers to abandon what can be a very helpful tool for guiding their minds, souls and spirits to a place that has eternal benefits. So, I wrote this with folks like this (and me) in mind.

This book contains 80 devotions. You have now been given permission to engage these devotions over 80 days or 80 weeks or any (somewhat regular) interval that feeds your relationships. Some people may choose to read and reflect on the content everyday, every few days, once a week or simply whenever they can. So, choose a frequency that can fit your definition of success! Your measure of success may be to simply feel more connected as a couple no matter how dusty this book cover gets. Whichever frequency you land on, decide now to make a commitment that you can stick to. Then, start engaging deeply and regularly with God and your partner!

As a marriage counselor, I am reminded regularly that when our relationship is in a state of tension or conflict, we are drawn to the negative. Focusing on what frustrates us about our partner and what is *not* working in our relationship negatively influences our attitude and outlook. If we begin a day with a belief that it will be a bad day, guess what will happen? With our amazing minds, we create what we believe and can become very stuck. In these pessimistic moments, we are in dire need of counterarguments. Alternative beliefs and a small, accessible collection of positive, truth-filled phrases redirect us when our thoughts start heading down the negative pathway. And every time we head off negative thinking at the path, we build confidence! We feel good about our self-control and ability to make positive choices.

We must engage the power of God to hear refreshing truths and overcome our tainted perspectives. Thankfully, everyday God gives us the gift of opportunity to meet with Him and invite His awesome power into every part of our lives!

Again, willpower is not enough. We need Spirit-power! As proclaimed in Romans 8:1-17, believers in Jesus have "life through the spirit":

> *Therefore, there is now no condemnation for those who are in Christ Jesus, because through Christ Jesus the law of the Spirit who gives life has set you free from the law of sin and death. For what the law was powerless to do because it was weakened by the flesh, God did by sending his own Son in the likeness of sinful flesh to be a sin offering. And so he condemned sin in the flesh, in order that the righteous requirement of the law might be fully met in us, who do not live according to the flesh but according to the Spirit.*
>
> *Those who live according to the flesh have their minds set on what the flesh desires; but those who live in accordance with*

the Spirit have their minds set on what the Spirit desires. The mind governed by the flesh is death, but the mind governed by the Spirit is life and peace. The mind governed by the flesh is hostile to God; it does not submit to God's law, nor can it do so. Those who are in the realm of the flesh cannot please God.

You, however, are not in the realm of the flesh but are in the realm of the Spirit, if indeed the Spirit of God lives in you. And if anyone does not have the Spirit of Christ, they do not belong to Christ.

But if Christ is in you, then even though your body is subject to death because of sin, the Spirit gives life because of righteousness. And if the Spirit of him who raised Jesus from the dead is living in you, he who raised Christ from the dead will also give life to your mortal bodies because of his Spirit who lives in you.

Therefore, brothers and sisters, we have an obligation—but it is not to the flesh, to live according to it. For if you live according to the flesh, you will die; but if by the Spirit you put to death the misdeeds of the body, you will live.

For those who are led by the Spirit of God are the children of God. The Spirit you received does not make you slaves, so that you live in fear again; rather, the Spirit you received brought about your adoption to sonship. And by him we cry, "Abba, Father." The Spirit himself testifies with our spirit that we are God's children. Now if we are children, then we are heirs—heirs of God and co-heirs with Christ, if indeed we share in his sufferings in order that we may also share in his glory.

The Apostle Paul's concluding exhortation to the church at Philippi summarizes the power of thinking and application:

Finally, brothers and sisters, whatever is true, whatever is noble, whatever is right, whatever is pure, whatever is lovely, whatever is admirable—if anything is excellent or praiseworthy—think about such things. Whatever you have learned or received or heard from me, or seen in me—put it into practice. And the God of peace will be with you.

Philippians 4:8-9

Our marriage and families are the greatest mission field. We carry the atmosphere that we create in our homes out into the world, into our workplaces, into our schools and into all our relationships.

So, the *Three Thoughts* are brief meditations that you will focus on each day: about God, about your partner, and about you and what you can do that day to help feed these two most important relationships.

WHO SHOULD USE THIS DEVOTIONAL?

Both individuals and couples can use this devotional. Actually, this may be the first "couple devotional" that works for individuals! When engaged with God, one person can create positive change, bust through negative dynamics, create lasting hope and begin to shape a new, loving marriage relationship. Dating, engaged, newlywed and long-married couples will find this material applicable to their relationship stage. Individuals and couples in a conflicted relationship may also find hope as they honestly examine their personal tendencies and relationship patterns while engaging with God to transform their relationship.

HOW TO USE THIS DEVOTIONAL

As mentioned previously, choose a frequency that will fit your reality and schedule.

This couple devotional includes two distinct days for each of the *40 Forms of Intimacy®*. If you need help focusing on a certain area in your relationship, you could work through that topic two days in a row. Or, you can move through all 40 topics two separate times. Either way, you have 80 distinct days to experience your relationship with God and your partner!

As you move through the daily devotions, you will also become aware of your relationship with God, insights about your partner, growth points for yourself and your own needs. So, take a few minutes as often as you can to (acronym alert) JOT down reflections, prayers and insights in a separate notebook or journal. Writing regular entries in your Journal of Transformation will help you personalize your process and evaluate your growth points. We can feel very encouraged when we record our prayers, hopes and dreams to later help us recall how God has been moving in our lives and relationships!

Some examples of the *Three Thoughts* could include:

GOD: engagement with God, prayer, gratefulness and praise, reading a scripture

PARTNER: focusing on a strength, gift, talent, quality, positive personality trait, aspect of her character, or a statement of appreciation

ME: a vow to start, stop or change something

Throughout this experience, remain aware of insights and revelations, strengths and shortcomings, victories and vows and struggles and challenges. Some of these writings may also become new vows you take each day.

When ready, you may share your JOT writings with your partner. As a minimum, you will Notice, Appreciate and Share on a regular basis. Be vigilant and remain aware of God's special revelation to you, about your partner and your relationship or marriage. Don't overlook daily opportunities to share what God is doing in and through you. Share genuine compliments and positive affirmations with your partner.

After you are finished with this devotional, start over again! Similar to when you read the Bible again at a different life stage, you may also make discoveries about your partner, your relationship, your relationship with God and yourself. And make sure to share anything you find helpful in this book with other important people in your life. This book could make a great engagement or wedding gift!

INTRODUCTION

IS MARRIAGE SUPPOSED TO BE DIFFICULT?

Have you ever said, "Marriage just shouldn't be this hard!" Or, have you ever thought, "Did I marry the wrong person?"

Enjoying a peaceful, connected marriage shouldn't be a rare feeling. Creating a close, connected marriage and repairing issues in a marriage takes work. A lot of work. And this is not a quick fix. The unpopular but honest message is that creating a great (or even a good) marriage is a process. It takes time, attention and effort. It may be uncomfortable at times.

If you began your relationship hoping it would look a lot different than it currently does, you may need to adjust your expectations. Having realistic expectations is different from lowering our standards. As believers we never settle for anything less than what God calls us to. And he calls us to live holy (1 Thessalonians 4:7), love deeply (1 Peter 4:8) and remain in Him (John 15:5)!

A relationship needs regular fuel. And both parties must clearly communicate to make sure they're not putting diesel fuel into a gas engine. And because we WILL hit some bumps in the road, our relationship requires periodic re-alignment. Since a relationship bond is living and dynamic, it changes over time and needs to be fed regularly. Without adequate nourishment, relationships will fade and die. As their default, our living bonds are dying right now! Therefore, it is vital that we expend energy and focus our minds and hearts on what matters most to us each day.

After God, our priorities must first be focused at home. We cannot afford to neglect the family God has given us in order to love others outside of our primary circle better or more often. We have to work on this loving thing and get it right at home first. When we struggle to fit in our most important relationships with God, our spouse and our children into our already-created schedules, these relationships will suffer.

When we get married, we think about how another person is going to meet my needs. Seldom do people get married to sacrifice for the other half of the marriage partnership. I still have not heard a couple in premarital counseling say, "I cannot wait to deny my comforts, sacrifice my needs and be content," all for the benefit of someone else. This sounds ridiculous, and in the least, radically counter-cultural! Yet, I wonder how amazing and peaceful this dream relationship would look if two people entered into the marriage covenant promising and living out such a vow!

In reality, we must understand that we are dealing with another human, who is also fallible, sinful and often may be difficult to get along with. The marriage relationship can be the most challenging and rewarding because there is a lot on the line. In no other relationship do we have the same breadth and depth of feelings activated (both joyous and grievous emotions) and the same number of roles (as spouses, roommates, parents, etc). The more we invest of our time, energy and hearts, the greater the potential for pain. And we will knowingly and unknowingly push our spouse's buttons.

But, as we remain close to God, pay attention to and feed our connection, we have potential for intimacy previously found only in dreams! I invite you to press into the fullness of the Father's heart and pray for wisdom, discernment and contentment. When we first invite God into our hearts and align with his truth, we can transform our own hearts and ignite a lasting passion into our marriage relationship!

> *Pay attention to your connection. Your thoughts and words have power!*

40 Forms Of Intimacy ® Definitions

The following list of areas in which couples can connect were taken from (and are fully expanded in) *40 Forms of Intimacy: Integrating Daily Connection Into Your Couple Relationship.* Each of these Forms of Intimacy are represented twice to make up 80 days of devotions.

1. Acceptance
Enjoying and bestowing peace by accepting our partners for who they are

2. Adventure
Enjoying a sense of adventure together through a variety of ongoing and novel activities

3. Affection
Expression of love and caring through words, actions and silent (non-verbal) interactions

4. Appreciation
Noticing and sharing what we appreciate in life, in our partner and relationship

5. Attunement
Tuning into each other by giving attention and being present

6. Celebration
Drawing attention to and celebrating achievements, milestones and feelings, both big and small

7. Commitment
A sense of deep security providing constant and underlying reassurance of loyalty and faithfulness

8. Communication
Feeling connected through open verbal conversation and non-verbal communication, improving our listening and maintaining unity through differences

9. Conflict
Enduring a sense of connection through working out different perspectives and preferences

10. Emotional
Recognizing, experiencing and discussing various emotions together while understanding and coordinating emotional experiences

11. Enrichment
Investing and spending quality time to grow and nurture our relationship bond in regularly planned intervals

12. Financial
Experiencing a sense of closeness while earning, saving, spending, giving and investing together

13. Food
Sharing a sense of enjoyment and pleasure through discussing, preparing and eating or drinking together

14. Forgiveness
Experiencing freedom, release and closeness from the ongoing need to freely give and accept forgiveness

15. Friendship
Enjoying companionship through sharing experiences and interests, and feeling mutual support, safety and stability

16. Fun
Experiencing a sense of enjoyment and pleasure while participating in activities together

17. Gifts
Giving and exchanging meaningful presents during regular intervals, special occasions, or at random, unexpected times

18. Health
Taking care of ourselves and each other to thrive physically, spiritually, mentally, intellectually and emotionally

19. Honesty
Striving to live with authenticity and openness by transparently disclosing the truth of thoughts, feelings and experiences

20. Intellectual
Learning and advancing in knowledge together through reading, discussing, and absorbing new life experiences

21. Interdependence
Recognizing our need for our partner and the needs we meet while working together harmoniously in all aspects of life

22. Love
Giving to, sacrificing for, and meeting the needs of each other through regular demonstrations of kindness and care

23. Needs
Identifying, sharing and meeting mutual needs

24. Outreach
Selflessly serving others and altruistically giving time, money and energy to support a cause

25. Overcoming
Enduring hardships, struggles and setbacks with health, family, finances, spirituality and other matters

26. Physical
Enjoying each other's physical presence through simply being near each other, and experiencing movement together through a variety of active, dynamic endeavors

27. Project
Enjoying a sense of fulfillment through dreaming about, planning, working on, and accomplishing projects

28. Recreation
Participating in regular and new activities outside the normal routine

29. Respect
Respect and honor through words, actions and treatment

30. Resting
Taking time to rest, relax, and refresh our bodies and minds, together and separately

31. Safety
Providing and sensing peace, ease, and approachability in our relationship physically and emotionally

32. Sensitivities
Identifying, sharing and respecting individual sensitivities, temperaments, triggers and vulnerabilities

33. Serving
Making life easier by helping each other with practical tasks and going out of our way to meet our partner's needs

34. Sexual
Experiencing sexually pleasurable thoughts, emotions and physical feelings, and expressing distinctly affectionate and welcomed touch

35. Sharing
Contributing to relationship closeness through disclosing thoughts and feelings and enjoying life experiences together.

36. Social
Building and sustaining key relationships with family and individual and couple friends, and participating in group activities

37. Spiritual
Sharing in spiritual practices and revealing thoughts, feelings and experiences regarding our relationship with God

38. Trust
Feeling secure about our relationship through believing in and counting on each other to be honest, present, loyal and reliable

39. Values
Expressing, sharing and merging feelings and beliefs that inform ethical, moral, social and spiritual principles

40. Visioning
Dreaming about and visualizing our future together, including how we will feel and what we will see and do as a couple and family

DAY ONE:
ACCEPTANCE

We must accept our partner as a whole person. We engage in a harmful practice when we reduce people into parts. We were not designed to be dis-integrated. Although we may experience difficulty in liking or appreciating certain parts of our partner, we cannot pick and choose.

One day this hit me really hard. I thought, "Wow, choosing not to accept my wife the exact way God made her is telling God that He failed or could have done better." Who am I to mess with God's perfect, wonderful creation?

Rejection is the opposite of acceptance. We all want to belong, be affirmed and feel valued for who we are. We want to know that we are good enough just the way we are.

We don't like to be changed. And when we feel like our partner is rejecting parts of us, we can easily feel as though they are opposing and devaluing us.

On the other hand, there is great freedom in acceptance! This belief should start when we say our wedding vows: "I understand that she doesn't have to be just like me, and I vow to refrain from trying to turn her into a male version of me." Thankfully, we don't have to be exactly like our partner to be a perfect match. Nobody wins when fighting against God's supernatural design.

It is frustrating and exhausting for the person trying to change someone else ("the Changor"), and it is annoying and defeating for the person being changed ("the Changee"). When we recognize that we complement each other through our differences, we have seen the bigger, beautiful picture God has created!

We must expect that we will regularly choose to approach something in a different way than our partner. If we keep getting stuck on a minor issue, this frustration is getting in the way of accepting and feeling connected to our partner. The person is different from the behavior. We must determine which behaviors are unacceptable. Neglectful, abusive words or actions that devalue people and produce pain are universally recognized as being harmful to the intimate bonds we strive to create.

Acceptance is for us as individuals to work on, not to demand acceptance from our partner. Ask yourself, "How have I tried to change my partner? Have I allowed some minor irritations or annoying quirks overshadow his true value? How can I let her know that I love and accept her just the way God made her?"

THREE THOUGHTS

GOD: Help me grow in praise and appreciation toward You and be content in my circumstances.

PARTNER: Reflect on and consider which aspects of your partner that you may need to accept.

ME: What thoughts and feelings rise up in me when my partner's differences surface? How can I show more grace and mercy in these areas?

Notes:

DAY TWO:
ADVENTURE

What do you think of when you hear the word "adventure"? How do you know when you've done something adventurous? Does your heart rate increase? Do you smile more? Are you thinking, "That was awesome! I can't wait to do that again!"

Adventure can bring us excitement as we take a break from the realities of life that can seem boring or mundane at times. You may have heard about the concept of a bucket list on which people begin listing all the things they want to do before they die or "kick the bucket." The great thing is that we don't have to wait until it is too late, and we don't have to pursue all our desired adventures without our partner. Ideally, into our lives we will integrate regular types of fun as well as introduce novel activities rather than let that midlife crisis or rearview-mirror regret sneak up on us.

Some of us may think that God wants us to live boring or serious lives. Your type of fun could certainly change after you choose to follow God, but it is your transformed heart that wants to switch. As Philippians 4:4 encourages us: "Rejoice in the Lord always. I will say it again: Rejoice!"

A sense of adventure sometimes comes from pushing past our comfort zone, trying something new and just having fun! Our confidence is strengthened, we feel empowered and we get a break from the perceived dullness or worries in life.

THREE THOUGHTS

GOD: I know You want me to be free and to enjoy a sense of adventure in my life and relationship.

PARTNER: What does my partner find adventurous that I may be hindering or forbidding?

ME: What can I do to help my partner have fun and make it easier for us to have fun together?

Notes:

DAY THREE:
AFFECTION

We can express affection in numerous ways. Physical affection includes hugging, kissing and other warm, welcomed touch. A loving, affectionate touch can release oxytocin and help ignite a deeper physical passion. Similarly, non-sexual, physical touch can also create a strong connection.

Reading cues and sending appropriate non-verbal signals assists in our exchanging of desired affection. How do you know when your partner is demonstrating affection toward you? Do you exhibit both physical and non-physical affection toward your partner?

Caring behaviors are also closely related to physical affection. We express love and care as we go out of our way to actively serve and meet practical needs that make our partner's life easier.

God clearly cares for us and is crazy about us. We are the objects of God's affection! His greatest demonstration of love toward us happened when he sent Jesus into the world to die for our sins so that we may be reconciled into a direct, loving relationship with Him.

THREE THOUGHTS

GOD: Help me strengthen my affection toward You and my partner. Increase my understanding of Your great love for me and recognition of favor in my life.

PARTNER: Which type of safe, warm and welcomed touch does my partner need from me?

ME: How can I express my needs for affection in more honest, assertive ways in which my partner can understand?

Notes:

DAY FOUR:
APPRECIATION

What produces feelings of appreciation and gratefulness in you? Sights, sounds, smells, words and behaviors can leave us feeling appreciative.

If you regularly snap pictures on your phone or other camera, you have a good record of what you enjoy. So, check your camera roll. What captivates your eye so much that you take pictures of it? Whether people, places, events or other images you desire seeing again, they are also likely worth sharing.

Viewing gorgeous outdoor scenery and witnessing a majestic sunrise or sunset make the list of shareable photos. You can certainly soak up that experience alone, but it is best when you can call someone (sometimes anyone) over: "You have to come check this out!" Appreciation was not intended to be enjoyed alone. We have a longing to share something beautiful with people around us, especially those we love. You know this is true if you have ever thought: "Oh, I wish she was here to see this!"

When we share our positive feelings with friends and family—especially our partner or spouse—we are letting them in. We are establishing a connection as we share our sense of appreciation wth others and seek to create a similar experience in them. It's easy to see that God had our relationships in mind when He created our eyes and the countless beautiful sights to see and share.

Appreciating God during difficult circumstances may not be our first thought. We may have to look harder to see the good. Even in difficult times, however, Psalm 69:30 reminds us that we can "praise God's name in song and glorify him with thanksgiving." Holding onto our faith and turning our attention to God and the people he placed in our lives can remind us of His sovereignty.

THREE THOUGHTS

GOD: Thank You for providing beauty in Your creation in the nature outdoors and in the people with whom You have surrounded me!

PARTNER: How can I share positive thoughts and compliments more readily and with more frequency?

ME: What am I grateful for that I can begin adding to a daily gratitude list?

Notes:

DAY FIVE:
ATTUNEMENT

Paying adequate attention and being present are difficult tasks. Speakers often ask for your undivided attention. They want to make sure that something changes in you as a result of hearing their message. And they know that you will not be impacted if you are mentally absent.

Our full presence communicates that we care and are there. It demonstrates that the person speaking actually matters to us in that moment. Multitasking is a highly-valued practice in the American culture, but our engaged presence is vital when it comes to our most important relationships.

Legitimate bids for attention by our romantic partner are not usually scripted. We must be flexible and open to answering those calls from people we love. We can't settle for convenient or drive-thru love. We must slow down and at times apply the brakes to stop! If not, missed opportunities to experience a sense of intimacy with our partner can pile up, leaving us feeling disconnected and dissatisfied in our relationship.

Many people in a position of struggle have stated that they don't believe their partner sees them as a high enough priority. Ask yourself, "Have I tuned out my partner because I know what she is going to say, or I'm just not that interested? Does my partner need more eye contact and for me to let him finish his sentences?"

We tune into and stay dialed in to what matters to us. Engaging God's presence can be a great way to kick start building presence in your romantic relationship. Create personal time with Him and find rest today!

THREE THOUGHTS

GOD: "Where can I go from Your Spirit? Where can I flee from Your presence? If I go up to the heavens, You are there; if I make my bed in the depths, You are there" (Psalm 139:7-8).

PARTNER: Does my partner seem satisfied with the amount of time and attention and focused engagement that I give him or her?

ME: How can I be more aware of and answer my partner's calls for attention?

Notes:

DAY SIX:
CELEBRATION

How do you make time to celebrate events, big and small? Celebrating anniversaries and milestones helps keep life enjoyable! We experience positive feelings as we look forward to significant dates and upcoming celebrations.

Which traditions from your childhood have you chosen to continue recognizing and celebrating? Have you introduced any new traditions into your relationship? We profess that events and dates are special to us when we draw attention to them and make our participation a priority. Taking opportunities to celebrate special occasions helps us feel close to our partner.

We can feel a joint sense of pride and connection when we hold a shared meaning around family and religious traditions. Gathering and engaging in special activities during holidays and other significant events produces positive feelings and amplifies a greater purpose. Celebrating among people in addition to your partner can also increase enjoyment as you help spread the love and recognition for the holiday or ritual.

Be vigilant to opportunities in which you and your partner can celebrate and enjoy a sense of closeness.

THREE THOUGHTS

GOD: Help me open my eyes to see and celebrate You and everything You are about.

PARTNER: Which holidays or traditions do my partner really enjoy and find important?

ME: How can I acknowledge and celebrate our significant anniversary dates on a monthly basis?

Notes:

DAY SEVEN:
COMMITMENT

What comes to mind when you hear the word "commitment"? Do you feel a sense of security, or does this life-altering endeavor seem scary? Do you feel vulnerable or safe?

Fear and anxiety from the paralyzing two-word question, "What if?" can have us worrying if our partner will let us down or might do something that creates unbearable pain.

Handing over control to God and another imperfect human can be one of the most difficult tasks in life. Previous instances of broken trust can harm our abilities to trust again.

However, when we are equally yoked in our foundational beliefs, we can find more security, stability and simplicity when we envision our future together. We can predict with greater accuracy the areas that will get us off track and have hope that we can endure the expected problems in life. Our shared values strengthen our sense of commitment.

To remain committed, we must hold proper expectations and make reasonable adjustments along the way. Viewing our marriage commitment like a marathon, we persevere to the end despite resistance and when it doesn't make sense to continue because of the decision we made in advance to finish the race! But finishing is not enough. More than just proclaiming survival, I believe many of us want to report at our 50-year anniversaries, "We had ups and downs but we are intimately connected because of our relentless pursuit of each other and enduring commitment to remain together until our last days on this earth!"

Every morning we have new opportunities to strengthen our commitment by recalling the reasons we got together and restating the vows we made. What will you do this morning?

THREE THOUGHTS

GOD: Your desire for a committed married couple is to become and remain one flesh. Help me to see and live my relationship in a way that brings You glory (Read Matthew 19:5-6.)

PARTNER: Consider how your partner views your sense of commitment. What demonstrates to him or her that you are fully committed?

ME: Do I need to renew my commitment to God and my partner? What does that look like for me right now?

Notes:

DAY EIGHT:
COMMUNICATION

It's not surprising that communication issues are among the top few reasons that couples seek counseling. What we say and how we communicate it matters! Whether it's our hurtful words or absent silence, what we say or don't say significantly impacts our partner. We desire that our most important person will understand and really "get" us. Assuming and expecting mind-reading usually doesn't work well. Alternatively, healthy communication includes a two-way process that demands an even exchange.

As two different people with two unique experiences in life, we are bound to have misunderstandings and step on each other's toes. You likely have a different communication style than your partner. So, when and how does your communication go well and not?

Our communication patterns are worth examining, and this requires slowing down and sorting out our feelings. When we have differences in this area, we must be flexible. Understanding and adapting to each other's pace and processing speed is vital. And we each must respectfully, assertively speak our thoughts, feelings and needs. This is resentment prevention at its best!

Again, we are guaranteed occasional miscommunication. Grace, patience and acceptance are essential so we don't get stuck and veer off onto two completely separate paths.

THREE THOUGHTS

GOD: Help me recall Your word: "Gracious words are like a honeycomb; sweetness to the soul and health to the body" (Proverbs 16:24).

PARTNER: How is my partner's style and comfort level in communication different than mine? Do I give enough space and time for him or her to process a thought and formulate a response?

ME: I vow to be more patient, flexible and understanding of our different communication styles. I will engage in verbal and nonverbal communication that will help my partner understand me better.

Notes:

DAY NINE:
CONFLICT

Conflict and disagreement are inevitable. Of course, how we handle these times is what matters most. You have a choice to be allies or enemies during those moments of tension and distance. I don't have to ask if you've ever been in conflict with your partner. If you have been together more than a few months, my guess is you are thinking about an example of a negative interaction right now!

Trigger points can prompt feelings of pain that can turn into anger, which is still acceptable until the result of anger becomes behavior. People don't get arrested for experiencing emotions. Anger only becomes a legal problem when people allow their feelings to make law-breaking decisions. Of course, we can cross the line in our relationships in unhealthy ways that never reach legal levels.

So, when you get triggered, when something demands your emotional attention, what is your usual move? Do you shut down, attack back, go silent, withdraw or take revenge?

We all get stuck in cycles or familiar patterns that can have us escalate in volume and tone and display unhelpful behaviors. When we find ourselves talking with the ALL CAPS button locked down, we're not very approachable! When we lose self-control, we may say things we don't mean or throw an adult temper tantrum that later leaves us feeling very embarrassed. Again, how we navigate our moments of tension and conflict matters. It is our individual responsibility to be aware of and improve our delivery.

You may be wondering, "What can I do?" You can take time to respond thoughtfully versus react impulsively. Consider pausing and connecting with the connection-transforming expression of empathy. For example, you might think, "Wow, she seems grouchy. I wonder what happened today. I wonder what he's really feeling? I wonder if she needs something?" We need to be curious about what's going on below the surface. Genuinely saying, "Help me understand" can lower defenses. This caring curiosity can beget compassion and help you understand what's really going on. Also, you can accept responsibility. Know and practice what calms you down. Think to yourself: "Will these words help or harm?" Even at the heights of my hurt, will my words and actions reinforce a feeling of hopelessness or hopefulness in our relationship?"

THREE THOUGHTS

GOD: Help me watch my words and remember: "Whoever belittles his neighbor lacks sense, but a man of understanding remains silent" (Proverbs 11:12). Hint: Our spouse or partner is our closest neighbor!

PARTNER: I wonder what he needs when he gets upset. I wonder what's really going on when she gives me that frustrated or disappointed look?

ME: What do I do when one of my buttons is pushed? When do I go too far? Do I hit below the belt or fight dirty? During which moments do I need to pause, take a break and engage carefully and respectfully?

Notes:

DAY TEN:
EMOTIONAL

We were designed to display tears as part of our normal human experience. So, where did you learn about emotional expression? Did you learn growing up that experiencing and expressing sadness and pain was healthy? Or, were you expected to suppress or ignore your feelings?

If we truly want to feel emotionally close in our relationship, we must first be aware of the tremendous impact we have on our partner and that what we say and do can create or destroy our sense of connection.

Since healthy emotional expression starts with adequate awareness, regularly paying attention and asking ourselves, "What am I feeling right now?" is vital. Especially when one of our hot buttons is pushed, we must be well aware of that next emotion into which we escalate. At times, we may very quickly shift from feeling annoyed and frustrated to getting angry or even rageful. Or, we may move from hurt to feeling down or depressed. We must ask, "Can I map out my emotional shift?"

In your relationship, do you ever feel that you are in different emotional time zones? As two different people, it is more likely than not that you will find yourself experiencing different emotions and engaging in distinct behaviors. In these moments we must be aware and share! Identifying and articulating our emotions doesn't always come easy for some of us. But we can only suppress our emotions for so long. If you have to go to the bathroom, that's all you can think about! Similarly, emotions will make their way out at some point, soon. We have a choice to process and release our feelings in healthy or unhealthy ways and at planned or inconvenient times.

We will enjoy a sense of intimacy relevant to how deep we allow our emotions to go. If we stay on the surface, our sense of intimacy will follow. If we take a risk and push past our comfort levels, greater opportunities for deeper intimacy can exist. If we answer our partner's call for connection more often, there may be fewer calls, or what we may sometimes refer to as "annoying interruptions." Emotional intimacy results from deep insight into, and regular expression and discussion of, each partner's emotions.

THREE THOUGHTS

GOD: Thank You for being an emotional God, for sending Jesus to exemplify appropriate joy, sadness and even anger.

PARTNER: When have I seen my partner feel safer emotionally so he or she can share with me on a deeper level?

ME: During which times am I least approachable? Is it possible that my partner perceives me as being judgmental or incapable of a loving, supportive response?

Notes:

DAY ELEVEN:
ENRICHMENT

How do you feed your relationship? What activities do you already engage in and what loving words do you already share that strengthen your love connection?

Many people engage in rituals that communicate love and demonstrate how their relationship is a priority. Getting your partner coffee and planting a kiss on the way out the door in the morning, sending a text message with playful emoticons or making time for a quick call help a couple stay connected when physically separate.

We care for and tend to the things we value. We devote time and attention to what matters to us. If the newly married couple does not take action to nurture their marriage bond, it will naturally fade away and may even die. Anything worth holding onto takes work and regular devotion versus rushing to the idea that "Marriage shouldn't be this hard. I must be with the wrong person."

Strong, loving relationships require both quality time and quantity of time. Our most important relationship gets tossed to the back burner and fades into the background by all the new things in life that compete for our time and attention. Raising children and building careers can still be done with proper planning and balance so that every important relationship and life pursuit is given adequate attention.

It is each individual's responsibility to prevent relationship fade. We may see the effects on our physical bodies from unhealthy food choices and lack of exercise. Unfortunately, the warning signs of disconnection and patterns of neglect in our relationship are far less visible. When pain and distance finally become obvious, a couple must take steps to repair their bond. Of course, prevention is easier than repair.

Prepare for the inevitable drift, disconnection and fade of happy feelings by keeping your love alive. As stated in the book *40 Forms of Intimacy*: "We are either feeding our relationship or we are watching it die."

THREE THOUGHTS

GOD: Reveal to me how I can make my marriage relationship a greater priority and take practical steps to feed my romantic bond.

PARTNER: How has my partner invested in our relationship, and how can I thank him or her regularly?

ME: I will plan a date during which we will plan our next ten dates!

Notes:

DAY TWELVE:
FINANCIAL

Do you combine your finances or keep them separate? Some couples maintain individual accounts even after sharing living space and creating a family. Although this option can seem to provide the most security and predictability, it can also feel the most segregated and dis-integrated.

You are likely aware of how your experiences growing up have affected how you view and manage money. And when we join our lives with another person, we learn very quickly about our differences in how we earn, save, spend, give and manage money. Earning money doesn't usually create problems when earned in a way that is consistent with the couple's values, that is, until the time spent away creates distance and leaves partners feeling like a lesser priority.

Saving money and denying some of life's comforts together can help a couple feel that they are on the same page. As they work toward joint goals, a couple's financial and emotional reward is realized and maximized. Spending money together with an agreed-upon plan can also provide a sense of fun and happiness. Giving money to others activates a deeper, longer-lasting sense of joyfulness. Whether giving to the church, one of their favorite charities or directly helping someone in need, couples can feel a shared sense of peace and a higher purpose in stepping out of themselves to invest into the lives and needs of others.

Paying off debt together can also produce a great feeling of relief. The person in debt remains in bondage to the lender. And this bond is not usually a positive one. Celebrate the freedom and sense of connection you feel in paying off debt! Whether a student loan, car loan or a mortgage, couples can experience great joy when sending in that final payment.

The phrase "In God We Trust" can fade in meaning when our government leaders don't seem to lean on God for guidance.

So, where do you place your trust? Our trust and security in our relationship and for the future can become unhealthy when we allow money to lead the way. We wonder, "Will we have enough? Can I trust God to provide? Can I count on my partner in the area of money management?"

THREE THOUGHTS

GOD: Help me to rely only on Your provision as I follow Your leading and discern my options to earn money.

PARTNER: How can I draw my partner closer to God, me and our family by acknowledging and reinforcing his or her strengths and talents around money?

ME: How can I be more trustworthy and a good steward with the money God has entrusted to me?

Notes:

DAY THIRTEEN:
FOOD

God designed us to experience pleasure. He gave us taste buds to sample a variety of flavors and enjoy one of the most basic human activities.

We can enjoy a sense of connection around food. We are meeting a very core need as we engage in interactions with other important people. People fellowship around food and seem to stay happy when there's food around. We talk and we smile as we load up our plates. And we usually know that food is delicious and people are satisfied by the silence of conversation after a meal is served. Life just seems better when there's food around!

Food, or lack of it, can also really impact our mood. We really shouldn't make important decisions or engage in tough topics when we're hungry. Food choices can also consume significant time and hijack our peaceful emotions. So, how is your relationship with food? Do you spend a lot of time worrying about what you should or should not eat? Is this struggle with self-discipline, old habits and giving into temptations?

If you find yourself and your family engaging in unhealthy patterns of thinking about and consuming food, consider asking yourself, "How can I strive to maintain balance to enjoy the great foods God has provided me but also make healthy choices?" Stepping into positive eating cycles can produce a great sense of relief. When we exercise, we are usually more aware of our food choices. And we are more aware of what we put into our body when we have invested time and energy into maintaining an exercise plan.

If you have the gift of at least one meal today, slow down and enjoy it!

THREE THOUGHTS

GOD: As the Creator of all things, thank You for providing me opportunities for pleasure through food flavors and communion with others.

PARTNER: How can I be supportive of my partner's food preferences?

ME: Could I improve on how to enjoy a stronger connection with my partner by waiting to eat together or planning and preparing food together?

Notes:

DAY FOURTEEN:
FORGIVENESS

Are you quick to forgive? Do you hold grudges? It's easy to see how holding grudges can perpetuate harm to self and the relationship. Interestingly, forgiving too quickly without examining the resulting pain and allowing the offender to take responsibility for the hurtful behavior can also be harmful.

We can release somebody—and even some system of doing things—without their ever recognizing a wrong. It is possible to forgive someone who never asked us to release them. Isn't that great? We don't have to wait for an apology in order for us to begin healing and move on! To release someone is to set them free. But the person who is harmed also gets set free.

Imagine the many offenses that two imperfect people can have as they blend lives and live life together each day. The possibility for miscommunications and offenses grows exponentially! Humility as well as recognition and confession of personal shortcomings are key ingredients for preventing expected human error from becoming relational offenses. Our tendency is to avoid personal responsibility and direct blame to another person. And our partner is a convenient target onto which we can deflect and project our issues.

We must become humble and take a one-down position to initiate forgiveness. As the person who has offended another, we must extend to that person adequate time to process the pain rather than demand on-the-spot forgiveness.

When we are stuck in a cycle of conflict with our partner, we can become very accommodating! We say, "Please, please. No, you first, I insist" as we highly encourage our partner to take the first step of admitting he or she is wrong. And then with a patronizing tone, we might say phrases such as, "I'm going to take the highroad" or "I will be the bigger person." We should genuinely reflect if these beliefs or phrases actual launch us into the one-up position rather than the humble, one-down position that a genuine apology requires.

Finally, we may need to eliminate the "I am sorry" phrase and instead more specifically apologize for the hurt that we caused. Most certainly we need to see our part in the harmful behavior, see how our partner was affected, engage empathy to join her at the same level of pain, and reassure her that we will not repeat that behavior.

THREE THOUGHTS

GOD: As I reflect on Philippians 2:5-11, help me really understand how You humbled Yourself more than anyone ever could.

PARTNER: Is there something my partner has done, and adequately apologized for, but I still hold against him or her?

ME: Do I take ownership for my contribution to negative interactions and specific ways in which I harm my partner?

Notes:

DAY FIFTEEN:
FRIENDSHIP

What qualities make good friends? Think about what happens when we secure, maintain and terminate a friendship. Why do people initiate a friendship, why do people seek to shift an acquaintance to friend status and why do people take steps to end such a relationship?

Friendships usually include some two-way benefit in which both parties demonstrate and experience actions and feelings that are encouraging, supportive and understanding. People seek to be seen and feel heard and valued. Friends are kind rather than mean. They are approachable and available. Close friends demonstrate that the other person is a priority for which they will drop what they're doing to meet urgent needs without pause or question. Friends seek to spend time together to nurture and strengthen their relationship.

So, should spouses be best friends? The previous paragraph would suggest so. Perhaps married couples were expected to be the original "Best Friends Forever" (BFF). Engaging in a strong, connected friendship seems foundational for the modern marriage. A married couple who remains best friends can overcome stressors, struggles and setbacks because they are stronger together.

As Ecclesiastes 4:9-10a affirms, "Two are better than one because they have a good return for their labor. If either of them falls down, one can help the other up."

Keeping God at the center of our friendship provides unmatchable durability since "a cord of three strands is not quickly broken" (Ecclesiastes 4:12).

THREE THOUGHTS

GOD: I praise You for sending me this great friend! Rather than try to change my partner, help me see those qualities with which You have blessed him or her.

PARTNER: Which friendship qualities in my partner do I most value, and how can I communicate my appreciation for these positive traits and behaviors?

ME: How have I allowed our friendship to decline? How can I be a better friend to my partner?

Notes:

DAY SIXTEEN:
FUN

Do you make time for fun? How often do you slow down to examine your routine and make it a point to disappear into fun, enjoyable activities with your partner?

If life seems like our only purpose here is to work and pay bills, we must examine and make some adjustments to how we spend our time. When under stress, we can forget to have fun. Taking a break from the serious and stressful issues we face in life is essential for our physical, emotional, mental and spiritual vitality. We can even become distracted from our devotion to God when we're out of balance.

It has been said that laughter is the best medicine. With appropriate timing and content, humor can act as the pathway to fun and help us relax! King Solomon wisely proclaimed that there's "a time to weep and a time to laugh, a time to mourn and a time to dance" (Ecclesiastes 3:4). Our smile enters the scene when we laugh and have fun. We lower our defenses and feel more at ease.

As 1 Timothy 6:17 states:

> *Command those who are rich in this present world not to be arrogant nor to put their hope in wealth, which is so uncertain, but to put their hope in God, who richly provides us with everything for our enjoyment.*

THREE THOUGHTS

GOD: Help me remember that You want me to have life to the fullest, which includes joy, laughter and excitement!

PARTNER: In which areas does my partner display and share fun and humor that I may need to support?

ME: Which steps can I take to lighten the mood in my environment and relationship and introduce fun and laughter?

Notes:

DAY SEVENTEEN:
GIFTS

Do you like to receive gifts? If you're known as being a good gift-giver, why do you give gifts? It is often easy to feel a sense of intimacy as we give and receive gifts.

Some people really love giving gifts. They may get excited about the process of selecting and concealing a gift, as it is the only occasion we should hide something or omit the truth from people with love. The special touches of the packaging, delivery and surprise of giving a gift all make the process special.

Other people need a lot more help, including time and inspiration and may experience stress as they search for a meaningful gift. It can be overwhelming when we scramble to secure a satisfying, last-minute purchase. Instead, thinking about our partner and purchasing gifts throughout the year can help save stress and anxiety around the area of gift-giving.

Although we easily link gifts to tangible "things," intangible expressions of love and connection can far surpass those gifts that fade away in interest or usability. The gift of your attention and presence through active, compassionate listening can demonstrate the most meaningful, lasting love offerings!

What is the greatest gift? There is no greater gift than love! God radically demonstrated gift-giving when he bestowed the gift of love, salvation and freedom through Christ. John 3:16 summarizes this amazing sacrifice: "For God so loved the world that he gave his one and only Son, that whoever believes in him shall not perish but have eternal life."

Reflect on the gifts that really matter in your life today and forever. You are sharing the greatest gift when you are loving and serving people. Be generous today as you share the gifts that produce eternal impact!

THREE THOUGHTS

GOD: God, refresh in my mind and heart today the power and freedom available to me through Jesus.

PARTNER: Which tangible and intangible gifts create the most meaning for my partner?

ME: Regular engagement with God, the original Gift-Giver, will help me recognize opportunities to demonstrate love and sacrifice.

Notes:

DAY EIGHTEEN:
HEALTH

What does health mean to you? When we feel healthy or perceive someone as healthy, our thoughts center around exercise, nutrition and well-being. But to be healthy means much more than to appear in good shape or temporarily feel good.

Our bodies represent only a fragment of our overall being. To engage our minds, move our bodies, express our emotions and connect to God to enhance our spiritual vitality is to play the instruments in a fulfilling life's symphony. We can be our best selves when we practice self-care and live a balanced life. We grow in confidence, feel secure and thus can show up fully for our relationships.

Being aware of changing health needs and making adjustments will be necessary as we age, decline in mental and physical ability or experience injuries. In unexpected, overwhelming seasons, our priorities will matter more than ever. We must stay engaged with God for strength, hope and wisdom to cope wth our emerging emotions and navigate unfamiliar circumstances and seasons.

Matthew 6:33 directs us toward the order of things so we may attain our best selves: "Seek first the kingdom of God and all these things will be added to you."

THREE THOUGHTS

GOD: Help me to connect with You first to develop and stay on track with a healthy living plan.

PARTNER: What does my partner like to do (or has been asking about) that moves him or her to a place of vitality that I can encourage and join in?

ME: How can I achieve a more healthy balance of spiritual, emotional, physical and mental health?

Notes:

DAY NINETEEN:
HONESTY

Honesty is an important structural component of the relationship foundation. There may be no quicker way to shatter trust in a relationship than deception.

Dishonesty shows its face through minimizing, omitting and outright lying. Even the so-called "white lie" can begin to break down trust and chip away at one's perceived integrity. One reason we may give for lying is to protect someone else, but most often we want to protect ourselves. Any time we feel a lie coming on, we must slow down to consider several outcomes of the potential harm and direct damage to our sense of connection with someone.

To manage an inventory of lies requires an amazing memory, especially when we tell several versions of a story to different people. We carry tension each day with the fear of getting caught in a lie. Most often, it's just a matter of time before someone gets discovered. The heaviness of a dishonest heart becomes a block to intimacy, but when we bring the dark into the light we can feel free and connected!

Authenticity is the antidote for the hurtful habit of lying. Transparency and authenticity begin with being honest with ourselves and examining our reasons for omitting information. We might ask ourselves, "Am I revealing parts of me or all of me?" Vulnerability involves great risk since it requires opening up deeper layers of ourselves that often touch the overwhelming feelings of fear and shame. Yet, the more we let someone into our minds and hearts, the more we feel known and connected.

As Proverbs 28:13 asserts, "Whoever conceals their sins does not prosper, but the one who confesses and renounces them finds mercy." We must take great care with anything that can get in the way of us prospering in life and our relationships.

THREE THOUGHTS

GOD: You are safe, accepting and merciful. Help me to begin confessing my dishonesty to You so You may refresh my heart and hope.

PARTNER: Focus on the areas you value in which your partner is authentic, consistent and dependable.

ME: How can I bring up a conversation with my partner to have us both move toward authenticity and transparency and being respectfully assertive?

Notes:

DAY TWENTY:
INTELLECTUAL

As a couple, we feel more connected as we learn and grow together intellectually. How do you keep growing intellectually? Can you recall learning experiences in which you and your partner have felt connected?

We can feel intellectually stimulated when another person shares our same interests. We experience enjoyable moments as we align our thoughts and share insights. Fewer opportunities for conflict exist during these positive engagements. As the joint focus remains on something new and exciting, couples can draw attention to the lighter, peaceful mood.

Especially in a long-term relationship and marriage, seasons may come in which one person seeks to grow skills and knowledge through specific educational pursuits. Changing careers or securing a higher or more satisfying position may be the motivation for this commitment. For whatever reasons a couple decides to pursue intellectual growth, hearing a clear calling to carve a new professional path should benefit the family. Couples can feel connected as they support and encourage each other as they reach their family goals.

It's easier to think of keeping our minds active by learning a trade or sharpening our career skills. Pursuing professional growth is required to remain current and continue adding value to the workforce. Although attending trainings may seem like an individual exercise, we transform a personal activity into a couple connection when we discuss our new insights with our partner.

But learning together can provide even greater opportunities to feel close to each other. Can you consider taking a class or learning a new language together? Perhaps creating time in your schedule to share ideas, opinions and feelings about a topic would help you feel more intellectually connected.

THREE THOUGHTS

GOD: Thank You for designing my mind to continue expanding with knowledge and wisdom.

PARTNER: Is there some activity or hobby in which my partner has expressed interest that we can learn together?

ME: Which of my intellectual and professional interests can I invite my partner into?

Notes:

DAY TWENTY-ONE:
INTERDEPENDENCE

Do you find it difficult to depend on someone else? Has anyone ever let you down, harmed or violated your trust? Perhaps the easier question to answer is "How many people have contributed to your difficulty in trusting others?"

Trusting and relying on another imperfect person can leave us feeling uneasy, anxious and even fearful. Speaking the words aloud that we need people can be difficult. It shows vulnerability and may leave us thinking that others will perceive us as weak or inadequate. Even admitting to ourselves that we need others may stir up these thoughts: "What's wrong with me? Why can't I just be strong all by myself? Am I not enough?"

We desire to be enough. And we are! But we were designed to be in relationships. Our Designer planted a longing in our hearts to regularly seek intimacy with him and others. He didn't want us to be alone. Knowing that we can feel more fulfilled and can function better together, we must continue our efforts to work together and maintain a healthy interdependency. With a track record of mutual support and teamwork, we can feel a sense of trust and safety that is matchless.

Very soon after He created the first person, God declared: "It is not good for the man to be alone. I will make a helper suitable for him" (Genesis 2:18). This helper was not a replica! She came fully equipped with unique perspectives and approaches. God knew that this man needed help! To remember that we exist to help and complement each other is to recognize a vital reason for our design.

THREE THOUGHTS

GOD: Thank You for creating me with the purpose to be in a relationship with You and others!

PARTNER: Are there some tasks or projects that my partner could use help with? How can I assist and be helpful?

ME: Do I need to ask for help more often to enhance our sense of intimacy through teamwork rather than choosing to complete tasks or projects alone?

Notes:

DAY TWENTY-TWO:
LOVE

How do you know when you feel loved? Does simply an emotion or physical sense of peace alert you? If you rewind the love livestream, what would you notice that preceded that feeling?

In many ways, the feeling of love is subjective and fleeting. Words and actions from another person can help us experience that loving feeling, but when that love is conditional, pain is just around the corner. Also fleeting is the the reality that when we enter into a relationship, we also assume a great responsibility. We are entrusted with another person's heart, and so we must learn how to best care for it and engage in actions that nurture its health rather than contribute to its pain. So, do you consider yourself a good steward of your partner's heart?

Denying our preferences and putting others first, making big and small sacrifices and loving when we don't feel like it seem to be less common expressions of love. We certainly don't see these uncomfortable realities on greeting cards! Yet, the most dramatic displays and deepest experiences of love happen at the greatest expense. Sacrificial and unconditional love seem illogical. More often we stop loving when it becomes difficult and when it doesn't make sense. We miss the purpose of love when we withhold it because we don't feel like it or when loving is no longer convenient.

Jesus provided us the greatest demonstration of undeserved love. He instructed his first disciples: "Love each other as I have loved you. Greater love has no one than this: to lay down one's life for one's friends" (John 15:12-13). Soon after, he presented himself as the ultimate sacrifice through his death. Romans 5:8 reminds us that "while we were still sinners, Christ died for us." As receivers of the greatest gift, we didn't do anything to earn it. And as believers and followers of Jesus, there is nothing we can do to lose this unending, merciful love.

If you have children, you want what's best for them. You know the bigger picture. You're ahead of the game. Sadly, sometimes we forget that God is our Father, who knows what's best for us and always has our best interests in mind. He knows how to transform relationships by continuing to love us when it doesn't make sense, and we can transfer this same loving approach to our partner.

THREE THOUGHTS

GOD: As 1 John 4:19 proclaims, "We love because he first loved us." (Read and meditate on the entire chapter of 1 John 4.)

PARTNER: Identify some sacrifices or times when your partner denied his or her needs. Verbalize your appreciation for those actions.

ME: I will ask, pay attention and continue directing my energy to what specifically helps my partner feel loved.

Notes:

DAY TWENTY-THREE:
NEEDS

Ask yourself, "Have I identified my specific, deep emotional needs? Do I clearly and effectively articulate them?" In other words, "Do I communicate this assertively with respect, or is it more passive-aggressively or aggressively in how I request that my legitimate needs be met?"

Our universal need is our desire to matter. We want to be seen and feel heard. We desire to feel valued, loved and respected. Perhaps more than anyone else on earth, we really want this from our partner or spouse, especially if we did not receive this type of loving attention from our parents. This unmet or under-met need may even bring up some emotions in you right now.

So, we must strive to be aware of and share with our partner when deep, legitimate needs are being met and feel unmet, as this empty feeling will leave us feeling tension and wanting more. When our needs don't align with those of our partner, we can also feel tremendous grief. We desire overlap but may need to understand and grieve the gap. This difference alone doesn't indicate that we're with the wrong person. Instead, as clearly and respectfully as possible, we need to communicate our pain and longings.

Sometimes we can place unfair pressure on our partner to meet all our needs. When it comes to our core needs, however, it's important to distinguish which ones our partner is designed and capable to meet and which needs we must rely on God and ourselves to meet. Our purpose for living comes from God, not people.

THREE THOUGHTS

GOD: I need You first! Every day I engage in relationship with You, I can feel more secure and prepared to interact with my partner.

PARTNER: Which three vital needs has my partner expressed that I can help meet?

ME: Which needs must I seek to meet with the help of God instead of placing unfair pressure on my partner to meet?

Notes:

DAY TWENTY-FOUR:
OUTREACH

The giving of time, money and energy seems to come more naturally for some people than others. At least, some people are quicker to assess others' practical needs, expend less effort and require less planning prior to moving into action to meet the need. However quickly the process happens, putting others first in thought and action is love demonstrated.

Generosity breeds generosity. When we see loving actions happen right before our eyes, we feel inspired! We can feel hopeful that great people do exist and will put others first, even at the expense of their own comfort. And often the blessing is mutual and multiplied. Many couples who serve in ministries and organizations or invest in causes that bless others end up feeling overwhelmed with blessing themselves. As a result, they can feel much closer as a couple! They entered into a joint vision to invest in a larger purpose to meet the needs and serve others together. But, in addition, they get to share in the special heightened emotions of love and service.

We find in 2 Corinthians 9:6-7 that the proper motivation matters:

> Remember this: Whoever sows sparingly will also reap sparingly, and whoever sows generously will also reap generously. Each of you should give what you have decided in your heart to give, not reluctantly or under compulsion, for God loves a cheerful giver.

Thus, we must give with the right heart and as we feel directed by God. Giving out of guilt and comparison or to manage a checklist are tainted motives.

THREE THOUGHTS

GOD: Thank You for Your truth and direction. I will meditate on this: "It is more blessed to give than to receive" (Acts 20:35).

PARTNER: How has your partner reached out to serve and be a blessing to others?

ME: How often do I share with her that I love her heart, her giving and caring spirit, or gift of hospitality?

Notes:

DAY TWENTY-FIVE:
OVERCOMING

Most of us have experienced some sense of grief in our lives. The painful emotions resulting from romantic rejection, a loss of a job, health and financial hardships or the death of a loved one can be overwhelming.

Undergoing challenging circumstances, navigating significant losses or recovering from a traumatic event may be the only occasions some of us access and share our deepest emotions. Staying connected while grieving may feel challenging for some people.

Sadness, hopelessness, fear and shame can prompt us to isolate rather than engage with God and others. We either internalize or externalize these overwhelming emotions. It's common to hear from a child: "I have only seen my dad cry when his father died or after he lost his job." Our emotional response corresponds to the meaning we attach to our loss and our most comfortable depth and display of emotional expression.

Therefore, we must slow down, be patient and express continuous love and care as we seek to understand another person's emotional experience. Often, our most effective response to someone hurting is simply being there. As a couple, we connect through the grief experience by feeling heard, validated, loved and cared for. To be held and hugged is also very important for some people. Overall, remembering that we are on the same team when we face unavoidable hardships helps us stay connected.

As believers, we have already inherited the supernatural strength that positions us to overcome loss, tragedy and hopelessness. Our power is exemplified through our faith. As 1 John 5:4 asserts:

> For everyone born of God overcomes the world. This is the victory that has overcome the world, even our faith. Who is it that overcomes the world? Only the one who believes that Jesus is the Son of God.

Paul also exhorted believers to hold onto a hope that extends far beyond our present perspective. In 2 Corinthians 4:8-9, he proclaims:

> We are hard pressed on every side, but not crushed; perplexed, but not in despair; persecuted, but not abandoned; struck down, but not destroyed.

As we persevere through the pain, and find something and someone to hold onto, we keep going because we maintain a sense of hope that we will get better!

THREE THOUGHTS

GOD: Thank You for being my Light and my Hope when I struggle to believe that my feelings and circumstances will improve.

PARTNER: Does my partner need greater sensitivity, compassion and understanding when he or she is processing a loss?

ME: Even before I feel like it, I will engage God's transforming power to overcome pain and loss.

Notes:

DAY TWENTY-SIX:
PHYSICAL

Physical intimacy is the feeling we get when we are physically near someone. This sense of closeness is not exclusive to sex. We can feel intimacy through peaceful proximity and by engaging in exercise with or near each other.

This form of intimacy includes sharing space and spending time together and apart. It is very possible to still feel close when we are physically apart. When our relationship is in a good place, we carry that sense of security and peacefulness into other environments. Sharing space and simply being together provides clear signs of connection. In addition, we can continue this sense of intimacy as we focus on positive aspects about our partner, recall fun experiences and draw attention to our connection even while physically distant.

For many people, the first day of the year prompts them to step into a new routine. With renewed energy and motivation, couples can provide mutual support and inspire each other. Talking about clear expectations, They can help each other get back on track and be each other's best cheerleader. Physical exercise can positively affect our minds and our moods, and thus, creates a comfortable temperature in our relationship.

Therefore, couples can experience positive feelings as they encourage each other and give and receive emotional support to stay healthy and balanced.

THREE THOUGHTS

GOD: You want me to move and not be stagnant. Help me to hear and discern Your leading so I may be my best self.

PARTNER: What type of specific encouragement can I give my partner to boost his or her energy, hope and determination?

ME: I will recognize and share when my partner and I feel close by sharing space and by encouraging each other's fitness goals.

Notes:

DAY TWENTY-SEVEN:
PROJECT

As couples, we can get excited and feel close when thinking about a project, planning it, completing it and then enjoying the finished product. For my wife and me, feeling a joint sense of closeness when working on projects launched me into the ideas for the *40 Forms of Intimacy* book.

I have also realized how this area of connection has changed. As I have become busy with other tasks, projects around the house have not been the main types of projects that have kept us connected. Now, as I share with my wife the topics I speak and write about, we have new opportunities to feel closer. My wife is my biggest cheerleader, and I sense that she believes in me. Knowing she has my back, I feel a tremendous sense of peace and closeness!

Some of you might be thinking, "Work on projects together? No way! There should not be any power tools near us!" Planning and working on projects together can certainly be activities that challenge our patience. We do things a certain way, and of course it's "the right way"! And many of us don't want to be told how to do it a different way. Practicing patience while allowing our partner to share ideas without criticizing or dismissing him or her is vital. That is, if we desire to finish our project feeling connected versus conflicted.

Although our interests and intimacy preferences can shift over time, couples can maintain a stable connection if they speak regularly about what still works and what doesn't. Also, our openness and thoughtful consideration of our partner's ideas can also add great value to the process and final product.

THREE THOUGHTS

GOD: I am thankful that You are the boss, that You have placed my partner into my life and that I don't have to make every decision myself.

PARTNER: How can I be a better helpmate for my partner when planning or working on projects?

ME: I will make sure to value my partner by soliciting and considering his or her ideas, input and contributions.

Notes:

DAY TWENTY-EIGHT:
RECREATION

Do you seek and participate in a healthy balance of work, service and recreation? How much fun and enjoyment do you permit yourself to have in any given week or month?

We must all engage in activities that help us get a break from the stress and seriousness in life. For many busy people, to relax and enjoy time together is a rarity. Yet, slowing down to enjoy the pleasures in this life is a critical ingredient for enjoying a sense of closeness. During recreational activities, we usually don't have to be "on." We can relax our minds and practice being fully present with each other.

Whether down the street or in another country, a change of scenery can be very invigorating! Having a fun and special activity to look forward to can itself reduce stress and increase pleasurable feelings. We get excited as we make plans for a dinner, day trip, weekend getaway, weeklong vacation or longer trip. How wonderful it is to create a scenario in which the biggest decision is a choice between two extremely enjoyable activities!

In addition, recreation can and perhaps should be integrated into every week. Lack of time or money does not have to dictate whether or not you can have fun during the next seven days. We have a responsibility to recharge ourselves, renew our motivation and recall our purpose. When smothered in work, we feel out of balance and may resort to the mindset: "There must be more to life!"

We can experience the feelings of a refreshed perspective after enjoying some recreational time. So, integrating fun along the way can help strengthen our connection during times when life's stressors and overwhelming circumstances are out of our control. And we can plan recreational activities for this week rather than waiting for a week's vacation!

Alex A. Avila

THREE THOUGHTS

GOD: I thank You and praise You for all your majestic works! I have countless opportunities to seek enjoyment that brings You glory.

PARTNER: What does my partner find fun and relaxing that I can add to our schedule?

ME: To be my best self, I will remain aware of recreational opportunities and seek a healthy blend of hard work and downtime.

Notes:

DAY TWENTY-NINE:
RESPECT

How do you know when you feel respected? Does this positive feeling rise up in you when people give you their time and attention and make you a priority? Do you know when your partner feels disrespected?

How we are treated influences if we feel respected or not. In the couple relationship, showing empathy and validating is showing respect, especially when our partner sees things differently. We respect others when we take the time to put our opinions and comforts aside while considering those of another. We don't need to be in full agreement, but we can still be a respectful listener and engage in meaningful conversations that help us remain connected despite our disagreements.

You've likely heard this before, but it bears repeating because of its importance: "It's not so much *what* you say, but *how* you say it!" Sharp tone and facial expressions can instantly create a perceived loss of respect and value. Instead, slowing down to consider how our words and actions will be received by our partner is vital for us to come out on the other end of a tense discussion still feeling connected.

Revering and submitting to someone demonstrates respect. In Romans 12:10, we are instructed: "Be devoted to one another in love. Honor one another above yourselves."

Elevating others above ourselves is certainly counter-cultural and can be difficult. But, we know that we show up differently when we feel respected by others.

THREE THOUGHTS

GOD: I am thankful for the stories about Jesus in which he exemplified high honor and always respected others. (Read and mediate on Phillippians 2:5-11.)

PARTNER: Ask your partner about and practice the specific ways in which he or she feels respected.

ME: I will do my best to humble myself as I elevate others and exalt God to the highest.

Notes:

DAY THIRTY:
RESTING

Do you make it a priority to relax, refresh and reset yourself? Are you slowing down enough to see the mental, physical, emotional and spiritual benefits?

Just as oxygen, food and water are necessary to live, we need sleep to survive in this life. A rested mind and body functions at optimal levels. It can think more clearly, operate safely and feel more peace and relaxation. How many hours of sleep do you and your partner need? Even if these numbers are very different, do you need to make resting a higher priority? A night's sleep provides opportunities to have a clear mind, to thank God for another day and to feel a renewed sense of hope for the days ahead. Our productivity and outlook will be also be positively affected.

Taking short naps and even lying down with our eyes opened or closed can recharge us. If you have ever driven multiple hours, you know that even a brief stop to rest your eyes and stretch your body can be invigorating. But many of us may need to schedule rest prior to exhaustion so we may be more present in every setting. Not only can we present our best selves to our partner when refreshed from adequate rest, we can also feel closer as we rest together.

Of course, it's common for things to get in the way of our foundational needs. So, what competes with your resting and recharging time? To increase our relaxation opportunities, we can remove distractions and increase simplicity. You might consider establishing blocks of time during which you and family members avoid using phones, tablets, and computers. You can designate a drawer or closet to contain these items to resist temptations. Keeping the television and other electronics out of the bedroom can also help us sleep better and enjoy much-needed conversation and companionship.

Genesis 2:2 includes the first reference to rest in the Bible:

> *By the seventh day God had finished the work he had been doing; so on the seventh day he rested from all his work.*

Did God himself really feel exhausted? Or, did He rest to model exactly what we need to do in order to recharge and be our best selves? Matthew 11:28 guides us to the starting line:

> *Come to me, all you who are weary and burdened, and I will give you rest.*

Finding rest in God and tapping into His peacefulness during quiet times can be the most refreshing!

THREE THOUGHTS

GOD: Thank You for separating the day from the night and giving me opportunities to refuel and refresh my mind, body, emotions and spirit.

PARTNER: How can I support and encourage those things that relax and recharge my partner?

ME: I will suggest ideas and create opportunities for us to rest and have quiet time as a couple.

Notes:

DAY THIRTY-ONE:
SAFETY

We often think of physical protection and security when we hear the word "safety." Our physical safety is essential to survive. In many ways, the steps we take in order to stay physically safe are instinctual and tangible. We strap on seat belts and lock doors to prevent physical harm.

Emotional safety, on the other hand, is more difficult to navigate. Since emotional experiences can be very subjective, safety in this area is hard to measure and understand. Even with the same person, our sense of emotional safety can come and go. When we anticipate a positive, supportive response from our partner, we can say that we feel safe in that area.

Think about topics that are difficult to discuss. We may feel vulnerable and insecure when deeper emotions such as fear, rejection, inadequacy and abandonment rise up. In these moments, we need our partner to be safe. If we feel that we cannot bring up certain feelings or issues to our partner, we may not perceive him or her as safe in that area. We may need to slow down and request safety.

If we took the risk to share something vulnerable, and we didn't get the response we needed, it makes sense why it may be hard to go there again. If our partner responded with criticism or ridicule, or maybe didn't respond at all, we are less likely to share again on that deeper level. Instead, we await a loving, accepting and supportive response to promote further sharing and thus deepen our sense of intimacy.

Similarly, we need to be emotionally safe for our partner. If we find that we hinder deeper sharing, we may need to start or stop doing something to create a safe and approachable presence.

THREE THOUGHTS

GOD: I will ask You for wisdom to be a safe person and the courage and discernment to know what to share and when.

PARTNER: How might my verbal responses, facial expression and other nonverbal reactions make it hard or easy for my partner to share with me?

ME: When I feel safe, can I take a risk to share a vulnerable feeling?

Notes:

DAY THIRTY-TWO:
SENSITIVITIES

What happens in you when one of your hot buttons is pushed? Do you escalate and express negative emotions? Is your main move to push away or pull your partner into your experience?

This area of intimacy includes two meanings of sensitivity: feeling a sensitivity to areas, topics and situations that create an emotional disturbance and pausing to exhibit compassion to others' sensitivities.

When we feel a sensitivity in a certain area, our emotions are first to show up on the scene. Whatever just happened clearly got our attention and triggered something inside us. Our rational brain must catch up to process, evaluate and organize this event. This executive function then helps us decide our next steps.

Feeling vulnerable, insecure and inadequate is part of the normal human experience. We need someone to be there and to care. We desire to feel loved and valued, especially after someone has learned this intimate knowledge about us. In these critical moments, our partner's compassionate presence and actions can soothe or exacerbate our pain. Our perception of this engagement connects or separates us.

We all want to feel understood and know that we matter. Although not our partner's responsibility to heal all our pain, having this particular person by our side to console us when processing our most painful moments can lead to the deepest sense of intimacy.

Likewise, we play a significant role in helping our partner move through an overwhelming emotional sensitivity. Knowing what cues historical hurts and triggers painful emotions, we can begin engaging our hearts and demonstrating the specific empathy he or she needs in that moment. Couples hold the power to help soothe each other and are given numerous opportunities to achieve a deeper sense of intimacy.

When someone "gets us," we feel valued and connected, important and seen. The more we feel understood, the more we can lower our guard and feel connected. Since these needs are vital ingredients of a healthy relationship, both partners must communicate what helps them feel an increase and decrease in these areas.

THREE THOUGHTS

GOD: Thank You for making me who I am. Help me to change in the ways I am able and remember to seek You first to soothe my hurts and meet my core needs.

PARTNER: In which specific areas does my partner need my increased compassion, support and understanding?

ME: What can I request from my partner to help me feel better and more closely connected in areas where I am most sensitive?

Notes:

DAY THIRTY-THREE:
SERVING

You may have heard it said: "It's the little things that count." The seemingly simple acts of service that we can engage in daily can certainly add up. Most important, they offer regular nourishment for the living bond of love.

As one of our most precious resources, time gifted to others expresses love, care and priority. Serving other people is love demonstrated. Putting love into action by prioritizing other people is a mindset and action that we can exercise daily. With the day-to-day routine and when our partner really needs us to step up and help more, we can show that he or she matters by our giving with no expectation of getting anything back.

When it comes to service, it must be selfless. If we seek a balanced exchange, our bias will likely have our partner coming up short. The first year of my marriage, I heard a wise saying: "Expect nothing. Appreciate everything." This concise advice helped me realize that my hunger for praise was unrealistic. If I didn't hear a "thank you" or receive recognition for doing the dishes, I recall thinking, "Doesn't she care or appreciate me?" I had to examine my heart and motivation for helping around the house and the reasons I expected her to be my primary source of affirmation.

In Matthew 6:1-4, Jesus encourages us to reflect on our humility and motivation as we give to others. When we remain focused on people noticing and praising us, we must check our heart and purpose for giving and serving.

THREE THOUGHTS

GOD: Thank You, God, for sharing timeless wisdom through Your examples that far surpass my vision and purposes when helping others.

PARTNER: Reflect on and share with your partner how he or she gives to and serves you, your family and others in ways that you find attractive.

ME: In which areas have I stopped serving my partner or spouse that I can restart?

Notes:

DAY THIRTY-FOUR:
SEXUAL

We should lust after our spouse! One spouse in Song of Songs 4:11 reveals: "Your lips drop sweetness as the honeycomb, my bride; milk and honey are under your tongue." Talk about a visual! Whether or not poetry launches from your own tongue, this brief passage illustrates an appropriately focused passion for the wedded couple.

However, this type of acceptable lust seems to be emotionally and romantically focused rather than physically driven. Becoming obsessed with the flesh, we forget about the heart. Yet, emotions naturally show up during sex. Our sensitivities and triggers based on our individual histories, unhelpful myths and inaccurate media messages can create feelings of fear, shame, anxiety, judgment, fear and insecurity. Therefore, we must approach our partner's feelings and boundaries with gentleness and respect.

In reality, sex may not feel as intimate or satisfying for both partners at the same time, an orgasm may not (and in many cases, cannot) be reached every time and the desired frequency of sex can vary significantly. Additionally, there is no single pathway to perfect sex, and individual results will vary! We must also expect and prepare to handle natural struggles. Obsessing about vaginal dryness or premature ejaculation may create those exact conditions. Our naturally integrated thoughts, emotions and body responses cannot be separated so easily. So, we need to be fully present and keep it safe as we discuss these vulnerable areas.

Using pornography as a way to enhance sexual intimacy directly opposes the perfect purpose and monogamous design for this sacred marital activity. Even if agreed upon, the unrealistic expectations and harmful fantasies created by viewing pornography can leave partners feeling insecure, jealous, inadequate, used and violated. Actually, engaging in any sexual thought or activity outside of that which is discussed and mutually accepted can affect both partners and the security of the marriage bond.

Genesis 2:24 discusses how a man and his wife "become one flesh." Of course, sex is required for procreation. But, the numerous possible sensations the physical body is capable of feeling demonstrates that sex was created for enjoyment in a secure, trusting bond of marriage!

God purposely designed our bodies to enjoy intense physical pleasure. So, grab your spouse (gently and respectfully, of course) and make conversations happen. This topic is definitely worth discussing and enhancing!

THREE THOUGHTS

GOD: You clearly care about both the sacredness of our marriage and our sense of physical pleasure. Given our desires and sensitivities, help my spouse and me enjoy deeper sexual intimacy.

PARTNER: What does my partner need from me to feel safe enough to share his or her specific emotions, sexual preferences and vulnerabilities?

ME: What do I need from my partner to share more readily and deeply for the purpose of enhancing our sexual pleasure?

Notes:

DAY THIRTY-FIVE:
SHARING

Did you get into a relationship to share your life with someone? How well do you share? Do you and your partner feel satisfied with the amount and depth of sharing?

Many of us want to be known deeply by at least one other person. As recently mentioned, Genesis 2:24 defines the married couple as "one flesh." Who better than one's spouse should the married person feel connected to? But even as adults, we don't always share well. We like our space. While driving down the road, we take ownership of our immediate area. We feel tense if somebody moves into *our* lane without sufficient warning. And what is your reaction when somebody cuts in front of you when standing in line?

Deciding to marry our partner demonstrates our deepest, lasting commitment. And so we must let them into our physical, emotional, mental and spiritual space. Still, sharing is vulnerable. Dropping our guard and lowering our walls, we are taking a risk, denying our comfort and abandoning full predictability. Inviting people into our minds and hearts grants them access to either help us feel safe and valued or harmed and disregarded. At these times, our sharing turns toward identification and communication of pain and the requested actions to repair the hurt. Specific, consistent and transparent sharing after an injury strengthens confidence and begins to build trust.

It's easy to show our surface (or secondary) emotions. People usually know if we're angry or sad by our tone, volume, facial expressions and other actions. Yet, even we may lack insight into what we're really feeling and needing. Before we can share deeply and request a safe response from our partner, we first need to slow down and access what is happening inside us. Our sense of safety allows us to become vulnerable. And then our feelings of anxiety, fear and uncertainty are relieved as we perceive continued safety after taking courageous risks.

THREE THOUGHTS

GOD: You have demonstrated the greatest selfless acts by creating me and inviting me to share in abundant opportunities to experience love, hope and peace.

PARTNER: Does my partner need me to be more approachable, flexible and graceful in my responses to facilitate deeper, more frequent sharing?

ME: How can I share more or less often and with greater depth? Here, quality with depth may supersede quantity.

Notes:

DAY THIRTY-SIX:
SOCIAL

Are you and your partner satisfied with the amount of time you spend together and apart? How do you handle your differences and preferences for more or less time together and with others?

You probably already know where you and your partner stand on the extrovert-introvert continuum. One of you may strongly prefer being with other people and large groups more often, whereas the other may highly value time by yourself and with small groups. How do you close the gap on these variances? Can you discuss and accept these differences instead of allowing them to launch you into a cycle of conflict that results in emotional distance?

Engaging in occasional conversations about how we manage this tension is important. A relationship thrives when partners feel heard and their uniqueness is valued and respected. Personality style and preferences are significant contributing factors to whether a person feels a drain or boost of energy while around other people. Such disparities may require more introverted partners to stretch beyond their comfort level to stay socially plugged in while accommodating their partner. Likewise, the more socially energetic partner may need to examine the family schedule and consider reducing the number of social activities. Although compromising creates mutual satisfaction, it does not always feel comfortable. Further, the expectation for both parties to get their way fifty percent of the time in every compromise is unrealistic. More often, we move toward our partner's direction and hope we're not the only person moving.

A more intimate togetherness can happen when a couple's time is well-balanced with separateness. We can be our best selves when our social time is balanced with other people.

Although some activities will be enjoyable to do together every time, others may feel more satisfying as we participate in them alone or with friends. It is common to share different levels of interest.

To remain connected, however, it is also important to discuss the specific people with whom we will spend time. Sharing adequate information invites our partner into another part of our life. Moreover, we must remain aware that the activities and conversations in which we participate enhance our faith and relationship rather than contribute to its decline.

THREE THOUGHTS

GOD: You are my highest priority. Fill me with Your supernatural measures of grace and peace as I seek a balanced life with my partner and others.

PARTNER: Invite your partner to discuss the benefits of a healthy balance of individual, couple and social time. Add some activities to your calendar.

ME: Seek to understand and be flexible with your preferences and differences so you may complement and encourage rather than compete and discourage each other.

Notes:

DAY THIRTY-SEVEN:
SPIRITUAL

How does your faith help you get through the tense, difficult times in life? Do you see your spiritual beliefs dividing you as a couple rather than uniting you? Wherever you are right now, try to take a step to go deeper in spiritual intimacy with your partner.

Examining life's deeper questions of existence and purpose alongside our committed life partner can help us feel a great sense of intimacy. Turning our attention to God—who knows all things and has our best interests in mind—helps us understand our identity and develop our sense of security as an individual and couple. Yet, one of the greatest blocks of engaging in a relationship with God is believing the lie that we have to be all cleaned up and have it together before approaching him. Jesus said: "My grace is sufficient for you, for my power is made perfect in weakness" (2 Corinthians 12:9). Thus, if we try to come to him already-strong and with all things figured out, we may be missing out on receiving His full power! It is no secret that God uses ordinary people to do extraordinary things.

When a couple humbly presents their individual and joint needs to God, powerful and life-transforming events are taking place! We cannot afford to miss out on knowing each other on this deeper level. If you're not praying together at all right now, have a conversation about how you can introduce this faith practice together. Prayers don't have to be all pretty and cleaned up or eloquent. As the receiver of those prayers, God knows your heart. But he wants you to speak the words to maintain a relationship with him. If you're praying already, talk about how you can take your prayers deeper and pray together more often.

Maybe listening to worship music more often and tuning into a Christian radio station will help change the tone and atmosphere in your car and home. Maybe attending a couples group at your church will help strengthen your faith and connection to God and each other. However, it's important to know that getting closer to God is not always about doing more stuff. He just wants *us* and more of our heart and devotion to him.

God knows both presently and eternally that we experience the greatest sense of fulfillment when having a solid and engaging relationship with him!

THREE THOUGHTS

GOD: Your Word says: "Come near to God and he will come near to you" (James 4:8a). Help me remember that You simply want me to engage You, as I am.

PARTNER: Does my partner feel comfortable praying out loud with me? What specific needs does he or she have that I can pray for in my own quiet times?

ME: Which faith practices can I involve my partner in that can bring us closer to God and reinforce our sense of unity and oneness?

Notes:

DAY THIRTY-EIGHT:
TRUST

How important is trust to you? Are you trustworthy? Is your partner? And which practices do you have in place to measure increases and decreases in trust?

Some people say that trust is everything in a relationship. As imperfect people, we will let each other down. But especially with our romantic partner or spouse, we need to learn and practice what builds and destroys trust. Trust is created through a pattern of honesty and dependability. When we can rely on and feel safe with people, we tend to trust them.

If we desire to remain in a relationship with someone who has violated our trust, we need to work toward forgiveness and reconciliation. Even for those relationships we cannot or choose not to restore through the reconciliation process, we can still experience great freedom through forgiveness.

Since trust is vital to our relationship foundation, great pain results when somebody harms or violates our trust. It seems risky and we feel vulnerable extending credit and loaning that person another piece of our heart. To restore trust, we need to see someone's heart in action and observe different behaviors over time. Rebuilding trust is certainly a process. We want to be able to count on each other with big and small things. For example, being consistently late when we say that we will be home at a certain time can start to chip away at the integrity of our word. On the other hand, being dependable reinforces the security and reliability of our promises.

In some way or another, we have all been let down by people, offended by their actions and felt the resulting pain, confusion and distance. It is how we reconcile that can bring us to deeper levels of intimacy in our marriage or any relationship. On the other hand, we also need to gain and retain trust in all things to reinforce our partner's sense of security.

When making promises to God, Ecclesiastes 5:5 states: "It is better not to make a vow than to make one and not fulfill it." We can certainly apply that wisdom to our marriage. We need to be careful when saying the word "promise," as it may unintentionally harm our trust if we cannot fulfill such a vow.

THREE THOUGHTS

GOD: Help me to value Your faithfulness, to be honest in all I say and to remain pure in heart and motive.

PARTNER: Extending grace to my partner is an ongoing practice. How has my partner been working to rebuild trust that I need to recognize and appreciate?

ME: In which areas do I need to strengthen the integrity of my word?

Notes:

DAY THIRTY-NINE:
VALUES

What is important to you? Pause and reflect on what tops this list and why.

Whether you chose all your own morals and values or adopted some from your parents or partner, you hold a set of values that inform how you live your life. We all have foundational principles that guide our steps and decisions. Our ethical guidelines help us navigate challenging situations and discern gray areas. Character traits, core beliefs and other qualities are inherent in our values and behaviors.

Naturally, we feel connected to people who think like us or can complement us well. Many couples get together because of their satisfying overlap in what they find most important in life. Virtues are values in action. So, they include expressions of positive qualities that are attractive to others. Consistent truthfulness earns us integrity, which is how we live out our stated values. Being honorable, people feel safe and can depend on us. They have nothing to worry about.

Are your core beliefs aligned? Alliance is very important here! Our values and beliefs show up early and often in our relationship and inform how we make decisions and spend our time, money and energy. Character qualities also influence how we treat one another and if our partner feels valued. If our partner does not feel like a high enough priority to us, we may feel tension and distance until we close this gap.

Overall, shared values give us greater opportunities to feel closer to each other. With openness and a safe connection, we also have an opportunity to discuss and realign our priorities.

THREE THOUGHTS

GOD: I will stay in step with You to make sure I'm giving attention to what is most important in my life.

PARTNER: Which character traits in my partner do I find attractive and help me feel more secure and connected? How can I communicate or compliment him or her in these areas?

ME: Is there an area of integrity where my values and moral principles need to be strengthened?

Notes:

DAY FORTY:
VISIONING

Do you have a vision for your relationship or marriage? Where are your eyes pointed?

We are headed in the exact direction upon which our gaze is fixed. Maybe you've never sat down with your partner to engage in deep conversations about the future and draft specific plans for your future together. Many of us enter into marriage with desired outcomes of staying together forever, possibly having children and being comfortable. We also carry the expectation that our relationship will last and simply hope for the best. Since every relationship will take on some shape, wouldn't you prefer to actively create your most important relationship on earth?

In business, leaders create a mission statement to declare organizational priorities and values. The accompanying vision statement names goals and initiatives to help express the mission. Further, a company's business plan includes strategies to clarify the path toward success. How do you define success in your relationship? First, we must know where we're going so we can plan how to get there. This process requires reflecting, discussing, visioning, implementing and evaluating. In marriage, this plan must also include selflessness, grace, flexibility and forgiveness.

As you might guess, a mission and vision statement for our marriage must also include continuous, sincere and vigorous listening! With more emotions on the line than a business partnership, our expectations must be realistic and remain flexible when life's realities detour our plans. So, we must create checkpoint intervals to evaluate and edit our plans. Remembering our sense of teamwork and agreeing to place judgment and criticism aside is vital for us to continue walking in the same direction.

How much better it would be to share a laugh while considering one failed part of your plan: "Wow, that part totally didn't work like we thought it would!"

THREE THOUGHTS

GOD: Help me stay in step with You as I recall Your Word: "In their hearts, humans plan their course, but the Lord determines their steps" (Proverbs 16:9).

PARTNER: Could I introduce to my partner the concept of working on our relationship's mission and vision statement?

ME: I will first spend time with God to know His heart and discern our future directions. I will listen to my partner and build flexibility into our exciting future plans!

Notes:

DAY FORTY-ONE:
ACCEPTANCE

What helps you stay grounded and hold onto your faith in the midst of uncertainty? How can your partner help you sustain your faith during difficult times? Can you recall when you have sensed God moving in your life in small, mundane and colossal circumstances?

Many circumstances are beyond our control. We may begin feeling annoyed, frustrated and angry at people and occurrences. The tension we live in as a result of experiencing things we cannot change certainly gets our attention. It can also become overwhelming and leave us feeling hopeless. When we recall The Serenity Prayer by Reinhold Niebuhr, we can refocus: "God grant me the serenity to accept the things I cannot change, courage to change the things I can, and wisdom to know the difference."

We often have difficulty managing the anxiety found in the gap between what we can control and those areas in which we have little or no control. Life is unpredictable in many ways. There is enough trouble going on outside our homes in this world. We need to do our best to feel a sense of unity and feel like we are on the same team inside our homes. Working toward acceptance can be one of the initial steps toward peace and safety to experience our home as a safe haven.

When an issue tugs at our heart, we might ask ourselves, "Why does this bother me? Is there anything I can do about it? Is this feeling rising up in me simply about my comfort and preferences, or is it about a strong desire for justice and peace?"

When something triggers negative feelings in us about our partner, we may need to simply move toward acceptance in that area. You may try thinking: "I need to start or stop_____." Or, "I accept this part of my partner, or I will work toward acceptance in this area."

When we release an issue that we've allowed to pester us, immediately we can begin feeling peace, freedom and connection.

THREE THOUGHTS

GOD: What do You want me to focus on in the area of acceptance that may be blocking my compassion for my partner?

PARTNER: Reflect on your partner's positive character traits that you highly value. You may need to communicate to your partner in a new way that he or she is excellent in your eyes.

ME: Consider how your choice of words and actions influence the peace in your relationship. Example: "I will be aware of my part in making our home a safe haven."

Notes:

DAY FORTY-TWO:
ADVENTURE

Adventure awaits us! We don't have to place our opportunities for adventure on hold and wait for the calendar notification. We can experience adventure in our daily and weekly schedule. Looking for both big and small opportunities to enjoy excitement together can become a new habit!

Our sense of adventure in a relationship can vary greatly. Do you like surprises? Does your partner? Knowing your partner's preferences is important. Both spontaneous and planned activities can be adventurous, but we need to be mindful and respectful of what works well and what doesn't.

Differences in how we approach adventure can also get us stuck. Some people prefer to plan events, whereas others feel an increased sense of excitement through spontaneous activities. Perhaps you slip into the roles of risk-taker and risk-mitigator. And one person's version of fun and exhilaration could mean anxiety and terror for the other.

Other times we don't have a clue what feels adventurous. It's interesting how we can get into arguments and really feel distant from each other when we get stuck in the "I don't care; what do you want to do?" cycle. Adventure is all around us, but we need to manage our differences and balance them well as we consider our deeper purpose.

God has placed adventure and movement into the hearts of his believers. In Matthew 4:19, Jesus was clear about the radical adventure into which he was calling his disciples: "Come, follow me," Jesus said, "and I will send you out to fish for people."

THREE THOUGHTS

GOD: Help me get excited about what You have called me to do and to share this sense of adventure with the person You want me to share my life with.

PARTNER: Which activities helps my partner feel close to me?

ME: Do I need to work toward a better balance of engaging in activities I would normally decline?

Notes:

DAY FORTY-THREE:
AFFECTION

Some people more comfortably display affection in public, whereas others prefer to hold hands, kiss and touch in private. Do you have a strong preference for regular affection? Would you rather not be touched? What about your partner?

Non-physical affection is powerful! Smiling is a universally recognized signal of warmth and affection. A smile can also communicate love, safety, peace and acceptance. Our partner's smile can place us at ease and prompt us to be more open. Engaging a kind glance with regular eye contact positively impacts our partner and strengthens our connection.

We can also feel instantly connected through verbal affection when our partner shares a compliment or laughs with us, takes the time to say "hello" and "goodbye" and calls us a special name.

God has an undying love for you! His relentless pursuit of you cannot be stopped. Maybe you're hearing this for the first time or need this refresher:

> For I am convinced that neither death nor life, neither angels nor demons, neither the present nor the future, nor any powers, neither height nor depth, nor anything else in all creation, will be able to separate us from the love of God that is in Christ Jesus our Lord.
>
> Romans 8:38-39

Claiming this truth prepares our hearts and positions us to share affection with God and others.

THREE THOUGHTS

GOD: Help me to remember that You are always for me, not against me and that You are always near me and love me.

PARTNER: Which types of non-physical and verbal affection might my partner be desiring from me?

ME: Being aware of my facial expressions, do I more often give looks that might be perceived as positive and accepting or negative and critical?

Notes:

DAY FORTY-FOUR:
APPRECIATION

What do you appreciate? More than when circumstances work in our favor and make life a bit easier for us, we have so many things to add to our gratitude list.

When we focus on what we are grateful for, we usually experience a shift in our attitude. Our positive feelings prompt us to experience a sense of joy, hope and peace. And when we invite someone into this matchless energy, we are literally "sharing the love." In our relationship, focusing on our partner's positive aspects helps us more easily overlook those areas that leave us feeling frustrated or annoyed. Every day we hold the power of choice to either compliment or criticize our partner.

A love based on performance will always leave people hurting and wanting more. Are you in danger of showing love with conditions? Actually, can any of us say that we never experience an increase or decrease in loving feelings directly related to someone's behavior? It's not a bad thing to point out positive actions in someone else to encourage that behavior to continue. This precise reinforcement is helpful for us to know what to stop or continue doing. But, to combat this ratio, we can be more aware of and share appreciation for who people are more than what they do.

Sharing a few kind words and regular compliments directed at our partner's unique qualities and God-given attributes helps! These life-giving words remind our partner of a higher value than can be attained by human effort. "No news is good news" doesn't work in relationships. We need to hear the words! As you recognize and share the strengths and value of your partner, remember to thank God as well.

THREE THOUGHTS

GOD: How can I look for opportunities to share my gratefulness about God and my partner?

PARTNER: What do I appreciate about my partner that I haven't shared and reinforced with him or her lately?

ME: More often, can I point out my appreciation for my partner's attributes and say "thank you" for his or her efforts that make my life easier?

Notes:

DAY FORTY-FIVE:
ATTUNEMENT

How well can you really tune in and listen to your partner? Do you operate at a different pace? Does one of you speak at a different rate and frequency? In an interpersonal relationship, paying attention and respecting pacing is critical. Think about those two words for a second: "interpersonal relationship."

Do you need to talk more or talk less? If you speak more frequently and quickly, consider slowing down to match your partner's pace. For some of us, our minds can travel in many different directions, process thoughts instantly and articulate ideas effortlessly. For others, it takes more time.

Often some very beautiful words and insightful thoughts can come from your partner if you just give him or her some more time—maybe even ten seconds, sometimes a few minutes. If you speak far fewer words than your partner, consider and share what your partner can do to make it easier for you to share more often.

We can hear but not listen. We can listen but not be fully present and engaged. Where do you usually end up during communication with your partner? Can you move one level deeper into more engaging communication?

Have you ever walked out of the room when she is talking and thought, "Well, I could repeat back what she told me if she asked" but weren't really tuned in with your presence and body language?

When properly attuned, we know what our partner may be feeling, and we care enough to stay present and engaged. As a result, empathy comes easier to us because we are in a much better position to consider her thoughts and feelings and track with him or her.

THREE THOUGHTS

GOD: "You have searched me, Lord, and You know me. You know when I sit and when I rise; You perceive my thoughts from afar." (Psalm 139:1-2)

PARTNER: In which ways has my partner requested that I listen, pay attention and remain focused?

ME: How can I be more present and stay engaged, tune in and not dial out?

Notes:

DAY FORTY-SIX:
CELEBRATION

We don't always need a huge reason to celebrate together. We can celebrate just because. Stepping out of the norm to enjoy a meal and date together can feel like a mini-celebration.

Recalling positive memories can help us create new memories together and launch us into a stronger sense of closeness. We can also get excited together about new happenings in our lives and in the lives of those people close to us. Telling our partner first about big news helps us feel close and creates a sense of shared success.

Likewise, personal achievements and professional milestones offer opportunities to celebrate. Perhaps your partner reached a personal fitness goal she has worked hard to achieve. Maybe he finished a big project or earned a promotion. Taking time to acknowledge and appreciate these accomplishments says, "I'm proud of you, and I'm happy to share in these positive moments with you."

The Bible is full of significant events such as feasts and other festivities that acknowledge reasons to gather and celebrate. We can learn a lot as we study ancient traditions and the reasons we continue to celebrate them. We feel closer to others when we participate in an event together that holds a deep meaning. Consider which accomplishments have meaning for your partner and you.

THREE THOUGHTS

GOD: I can celebrate with You through worship using my voice and instruments to bring You praise! (Read Psalm 150:1-6.)

PARTNER: In which areas does my partner feel special, affirmed and acknowledged as a result of his or her persistent effort and patience?

ME: How can I draw attention to and celebrate my partner's small and large accomplishments?

Notes:

DAY FORTY-SEVEN:
COMMITMENT

A relationship includes commitment, but a marriage involves a covenant! We miss out on the beauty and safety of the covenantal relationship when we project onto marriage the ideas of a contract, which outlines a conditional give-and-take.

A covenant perspective produces an increased security, accountability and more potential for deeper intimacy. A covenant is a promise that cannot be broken. So, we can have faith that the promises in the Bible that God has made to us as his faithful followers are ones that he has delivered and will continue to deliver on!

Further, a marriage covenant includes an unconditional promise that we will be there for our partner and will stay there, no matter what. We must honor our word. Although we can learn how to more accurately anticipate how our life will go, many things in life are unexpected.

As the bonding glue, our vows and promises we made to each other are in place to hold us together during times when everything emotional in us—whether it is feeling overwhelmed, anxious, afraid or betrayed—screams at us to abandon ship! The promises we proclaimed at our marriage ceremony help us endure hardships and unexpected setbacks. Such experiences strengthen our marital bond and increase our resiliency for what may come next.

THREE THOUGHTS

GOD: Help me to first understand my commitment to You. You are unwavering in Your identity and Your promises.

PARTNER: What does my partner need from me to build his or her sense of security and intimacy in our relationship?

ME: Which words and actions from me indicate to my partner that I am "all in" and fully committed?

Notes:

DAY FORTY-EIGHT:
COMMUNICATION

How do you know when someone is actively engaged when you are talking? Likely that person's warm, silent presence has indicated more engagement than the occasional verbal comments. Attending a conversation with our entire body is hard! However, listening with eye contact and maintaining an open body posture make the best audience.

Both verbal and nonverbal engagement is helpful for an intimate interaction. Demonstrating empathy and sharing validation are powerful interactional responses that communicate: "You get me!" and "You care about me!" Maybe you've felt this type of connection when someone places their life on hold to get into your shoes. With their kind smile and caring eyes, you know that they see you. Their engagement tells you, "As best as I can, I feel your pain, and I am moved by it. And I am here." Wow, we all need more of that!

On the other hand, miscommunication and misinterpretations can be frustrating, especially with our most important person. I really believe that the Enemy confuses our language! We can hear other people in the room talk, but there's something about tracking with our partner's tone and volume that requires even greater effort. Being clear and asking clarifying questions can help. You might kindly interject, "Let me see if I'm following you" on occasion to clear up an any crossed signals before either of you get too far down the wrong path.

THREE THOUGHTS

GOD: Help me be an even better communicator as I meditate on the biblical truth: "Let your speech always be gracious, seasoned with salt, so that you may know how you ought to answer each person" (Colossians 4:6).

PARTNER: In which ways has your partner alerted you to his or needs of being a good listener?

ME: Check in with your partner on how he or she feels when you show empathy and validation. How does your partner perceive your engagement when you are in the listening role?

Notes:

DAY FORTY-NINE:
CONFLICT

Whether reasonable misunderstandings, emotional battles or power struggles, relationship conflict holds endless possibilities to divide a couple that was once feeling peacefully connected and worry-free.

When our buttons are pushed and our defense system is ignited, we may easily access all-or-nothing language and declare absolutes such as "never" or "always." Adding "You" to our artillery introduces a stronger attacking element. Further, stacking up negative sentence starters including, "You always" or "You never" with "Why…" puts people on the defense and leaves them scrambling to provide a valid reason to defend their feeling of being accused or blamed. And the negative, disconnected cycle persists.

Blaming is a waste of energy that immediately puts partners on opposite sides, leaving both of them feeling bad. Have you ever exclaimed, "Well, you're the one…!" as you skillfully assign responsibility to your partner while completely ignoring your less-than-helpful contributions? From my experiences, many people have said, "You ruined our day, our weekend or our entire trip!"

Someone else can certainly color the atmosphere and impact our mood, but we each have an opportunity to call a "reset" even in the middle of the day. When used genuinely, "You are right!" can be a very effective disarming and validating statement. This statement indicates that we just might be incorrect. To be open even for a moment during times when you feel you are on completely opposite ends of the spectrum can close the gap and place your partner within a comfortable, loving reach.

In moments of conflict, the one thing we have in common is that we want the other person to take responsibility! We are often slow to consider the significant part that we play in disagreements. We might ask ourselves more often, "Which supporting role did I take and which dramatic script did I just read that contributed to this heated discussion?" We forget that we are on the same team and that when there must be a winner, there will also be a loser. Through this competition, our sense of intimacy suffers. Our partner is not the enemy. The Enemy is the enemy. We are on the same team. And when we access God's power as we accept responsibility, our mutual sense of intimacy will prevail!

THREE THOUGHTS

GOD: Help me recall Your ever-loving presence when I feel hopeless and distant from my partner. Help me to see my part, to be humble and remain approachable.

PARTNER: How can my partner begin genuinely feeling that I am on his or her team and know that I have his or her best interests in mind even during disagreements?

ME: Where can I give more credit to my partner than assign blame?

Notes:

DAY FIFTY:
EMOTIONAL

Do you ever notice a mismatch of emotions with your partner? At times we may feel different and distant even in the same situation. We may also get mad if a situation doesn't bother our partner the way it bothers us. We attach meaning and create powerful emotional and neurological associations to occurrences that impact us. When our partner feels similarly, we feel connected. When we don't, we both know it!

Although it helps when we align closely, we don't have to—and most likely will not—be a perfect match in the area of emotional experience. Our experiences in life are very subjective. If our partner assigns a higher emotional meaning to an event than we do, we must attempt to understand and validate the gap. We need not completely align and force an exact emotional reaction. Most often, our partner may need to hear a genuine validation statement that communicates: "I see you, I hear you, it bothers me to see you this way, and I am impacted by your pain."

It is very appropriate to say, "When you did_____, I felt rejected or inadequate or afraid." Of course, emotional openness and vulnerability can simply be scary! In these times, we may need help from another person to help us be safer with each other. Other times, we can just tell our partner that it is scary to delve deeper and agree on what conditions would help us share those vulnerable thoughts and feelings.

One explanation of why a couple stays stuck in a perpetuating conflict could be the very distinct emotions the partners each experience during the same situation or shared experience. We hear and see anger, which shadows legitimate needs. But what an angry reaction may be protecting is the core assurance: "Will you be there for me? Can I count on you?" We must be aware of and sensitive to when one of us needs to share these deeper feelings.

THREE THOUGHTS

GOD: Help me to express emotions in a healthier way. Guide me to be honest, loving and genuine with how I feel.

PARTNER: How does my partner need me to more accurately communicate my emotions so he or she may better understand my feelings and needs?

ME: Which emotions do I show outwardly? Do I show my partner deeper emotions such as pain, fear or shame? Does it feel safe for me to go deeper? Could I tell her what would help me share deeper feelings?

Notes:

DAY FIFTY-ONE:
ENRICHMENT

How much of your time, money and energy do you direct toward enhancing your most important relationship on this earth? You're doing it now! Sadly, you are probably in the minority of people who devote time to develop and strengthen their relationship. More than a temporary relationship status, staying engaged must be a daily practice and lifelong pursuit of a sacred emotional connection.

A loving bond is an active, dynamic and living entity that must be nurtured. Any thing we expect to stay alive requires attention. A neglected garden will be overcome with weeds, but a strong root system will help us thrive!

When we are securely connected in our most important relationships, the typical stressors and struggles in life seem less overwhelming. A problem is just a problem that no longer knocks us off balance or leaves us feeling hopeless. Our strong bond gets us through the tough times. Knowing we are on the same team, we can lean on and trust our partner to be there and offer support and understanding.

You hold the power to actively shape your sense of intimacy! Every month you can celebrate your anniversary. Take and make time to strengthen your relationship. Your investment in a relationship with God and important people around you is truly the best choice you can make in life.

THREE THOUGHTS

GOD: Help me draw near to You. You designed me to be in a relationship with You and other people. Reveal to me how You and others are my greatest priorities.

PARTNER: In which (maybe even non-traditional) ways has my partner put forth effort to feed our relationship in this past month?

ME: How can I honor my partner by scheduling dates that are fun or important to my partner?

Notes:

DAY FIFTY-TWO:
FINANCIAL

Has money ever gotten in the way of feeling connected to your partner? We can allow the very important area of money to create disunity and division in our relationship. Or, we can decide to discuss regularly and listen to the underlying emotions influencing how we manage our finances.

Power differentials and control can create negative dynamics that persist through the lifespan of a relationship. Our priorities, values and emotions are all wrapped up in currency. Do you worry about money? Some people might answer, "I don't worry about money because I don't have any!" We may feel anxiety if we feel we don't have enough money. But will we ever have enough? Actually, couples who manage money well and maintain a sense of gratitude for their portion may feel more content and connected, even when they have very little money.

Alternatively, we may spend recklessly if we have high account balances. People who inherit money or win the lottery can experience a range of unexpected, negative consequences. Spending habits can get out of control, and we may stop trusting in God for provision. Regardless of our account balance, we are called to exercise discipline and be good stewards with our finances.

The Bible states that we "cannot serve both God and money" (Matthew 6:24b) because only one can be your master. A master is one to whom you submit and give your trust.

Currency is necessary in this world's system. Humans have likely used some form of currency to obtain goods and services for thousands of years. But, people get off track when they elevate money above what really matters in life. As 1 Timothy 6:10a clarifies, "For the love of money is a root of all kinds of evil." Money itself is not a sin or inherently bad. The second half of the verse reveals some reasons:

"Some people, eager for money, have wandered from the faith and pierced themselves with many griefs" (1 Timothy 6:10b).

So, we must not only remain aware of how finances impact our relationships but also examine the influential pull that money has on our life and emotions.

THREE THOUGHTS

GOD: You are the Provider of all I need. Since many things in this world are insecure and unpredictable, help me to remember that I can trust You.

PARTNER: What are my partner's strengths in the area of finances? Can I more regularly share my appreciation of how he or she manages money?

ME: What does my partner need from me in order to feel more financially secure and stable?

Notes:

DAY FIFTY-THREE:
FOOD

Other than breathing, drinking water and loving each other, which other activities must we engage in regularly to survive?

Just like breathing, eating can also be an activity we take for granted. We pair eating with other activities as we eat at our desks and in our cars. And it seems that men are more known for their speed-eating. Slowing down can really help us taste and experience the many flavors in our food. Mealtimes can be great reminders for us to appreciate what we have and offer prayers of thankfulness. Some families have retained the family meal as an important gathering opportunity to share about their lives and happenings so they may stay connected.

Out of habit, sometimes we don't eat meals together as a family. It seems increasingly challenging to wait for each other and sit down and have a family meal. At the Lord's Supper, the Apostle Paul mentioned the practice of waiting to eat together (1 Corinthians 11:33). People seem to feel respected when others have received their food but still wait for everyone to be served.

Although life can become busy, eating together when possible can help a couple feel connected.

THREE THOUGHTS

GOD: Help me remember that my need to eat each day can also be an opportunity to commune with You.

PARTNER: Which food or meal experience could I prepare or plan that would surprise my partner and create feelings of appreciation?

ME: How can I slow down to experience the taste of food and draw attention to the connection opportunities with God and others?

Notes:

DAY FIFTY-FOUR:
FORGIVENESS

What have you learned about forgiveness growing up? How was forgiveness modeled in your household? We often carry memories and messages into adulthood. Two common misconceptions are that forgiveness should mean forgetfulness and that we have to wait for offenders to genuinely apologize before we can forgive them.

We pass some of these beliefs onto our kids. But thankfully, we can also abandon incorrect assumptions about forgiveness as we learn new and healthier ways to navigate relationship offenses. Forgiving is not forgetting. Many people would gladly take the pill that erases the painful parts of their lives. In reality, portions of painful memories can hang on for decades.

Although we cannot easily forget serious offenses, we will stay stuck at the point of unforgiveness. The very close siblings of bitterness and resentment can easily creep in, cover up the legitimate pain and restrict our intimacy potential. Thankfully, people don't have to apologize as a prerequisite to our choice of forgiving and releasing them! Unforgiveness often hurts us more than the offender. It can negatively impact our physical, mental, emotional and spiritual health.

Another misconception is that forgiving someone and thus "setting them free" communicates that their offense was justified. But we don't have to live in bondage of pain and bitterness. When we choose to forgive, all parties involved can experience great freedom! We feel free, our offender is off the hook and our relationship strengthens (if we decide—or are able—to continue the relationship). We can even release people and heal from relationship trauma caused by people who are no longer living or refuse to recognize their offenses.

God is all about healthy relationships! Matthew 5:22 instructs us to "leave the altar and go forgive your brother." Basically, God is saying that forgiveness is a greater gift than other recognized offerings for Him. Critical passages such as this one help us realize that God is more about relationship than religion.

THREE THOUGHTS

GOD: Help me see that holding onto unforgiveness affects my spiritual health and may get in the way of my relationship with You.

PARTNER: Which annoyances can I work toward accepting and release my partner from?

ME: In which areas might I be causing or perpetuating harm and disconnection in my relationship for which I need to accept responsibility and seek forgiveness?

Notes:

DAY FIFTY-FIVE:
FRIENDSHIP

Are you friends with your spouse, fiancé or significant other? If so, how do you know? And how do you expect to retain the title of "friends" as your relationship ages?

When we choose to be in a committed relationship with someone, we remain together because we'd rather be with this person than without. But we must work harder than ever to maintain a close friendship!

In romantic and marriage relationships, more is on the line. More emotions are activated, more risk is involved and thus more potential for hurt exists. It is very vulnerable as we are investing emotionally, mentally, spiritually, financially and so many other ways. We may put up our guard, avoid tough conversations and fight dirty in this relationship when we wouldn't engage in these same avoidant or aggressive behaviors with another friend.

We may enter into a relationship or marriage covenant hoping for a close friendship along with sharing additional benefits that bind us together. Our expectations may be dashed when we start to experience a breakdown in friendship qualities and sense that our relationship is in danger. In reality we may become aware of many differences, begin to drift apart and feel sadness and tension as we grieve that some of our needs may go unmet and that our partner doesn't fulfill all our hopes and expectations. We can choose to live in that tension and disappointment, always hoping for more. Or, we can begin communicating our desires, adjusting our expectations, accepting our reality and grieving our losses.

If you have begun losing your friendship, you may need to reflect on and return to the foundational qualities of friends. Friends are kind to each other and they nurture their friendship. They share compliments, communicate, forgive and serve each other.

In the least, we need to be able to count on, lean on and trust our romantic friend or spouse. We need this person to be there for us. Friendship starts with kindness.

So, are you a good friend?

THREE THOUGHTS

GOD: Reveal to me the ways in which I need to be a better friend. Help me emulate Your irresistible attributes of love, grace and peace.

PARTNER: Notice and share with your partner his or her most prominent friendship qualities.

ME: How can I become a better friend and be more desirable to be around?

Notes:

DAY FIFTY-SIX:
FUN

Which activities help you feel connected? How often do you engage in activities just because your partner likes them? Or, do you refuse your partner's type of fun?

Couples may exercise different approaches and make very diverse choices in how they spend their free time. If we wait to have fun only during leisure time, life may not seem much fun at all. Integrating and looking for opportunities to introduce fun into our work and when fulfilling other routine responsibilities at home can add to our ongoing sense of joy.

When seeking to introduce fun activities, timing and the state of a couple's relationship play key roles. Even when conflict exists and unresolved arguments are running in the background, engaging in fun activities as a normal part of the weekly routine can help ease tension.

What's on your fun list? How many of these items make it onto your calendar? More than starting a list of fun activities, we must make them happen. We miss out on tremendous opportunities in our 20s, 30s, 40s and well before our 70s and 80s if we do not make fun happen. In some of life's seasons, it may seem that we don't have the time or an extra dime to have fun. But there are many things we can do that require little cost of time and money.

We can always squeeze some fun into our routine. Have fun this week!

THREE THOUGHTS

GOD: Help me to see the opportunities for fun that You place before me and to enjoy a healthy balance of fun in my life and relationship.

PARTNER: Which types of fun does my partner need to relax and stay balanced, and how can I be more aware of timing when introducing fun activities?

ME: Which adventurous activities can I think about and add to our fun list in the coming days and months?

Notes:

DAY FIFTY-SEVEN:
GIFTS

How do you know when you received a gift? Aside from the fancy paper, bow or surprise delivery, when do you consider something a gift? Does the process of finding the right gift create stress and anxiety for you?

Today we can be overwhelmed simply because of the array of gift options. And choosing a gift for some people and in some seasons can be a task that leaves us feeling clueless. On special occasions, it is usually best avoid giving gifts that have to do with cleaning and cooking! But sometimes we appreciate and need practical household maintenance gifts or simply cannot think of anything else we would enjoy.

One year, nonstick cookware was all I wanted for Christmas! Not exactly one of those gifts you would jump up and down for as a teenager! Although my wife really has a better gift for cooking and serves our family in this area more frequently, I appreciate the process and product much more when I have the proper equipment.

To help generate ideas in the area of gift-giving, consider the 11 types of gifts:

Personalized: special, unique, heart-touching

Practical: useful gift that makes life easier

Private: an intimate gift that other people will likely not see or hear about

Proud: acknowledging an accomplishment

Public: given in the presence of others

Precious: original, treasured and deeply meaningful

Pretty: expresses and exhibits beauty in appearance

Perfect: thoughtful, uncommon gift that is a good fit

Precursor: the gift before the gift alerting recipient something else is coming

Process: builds excitement, anticipation and hopefulness

Prepared: saved for and planned in advance.

Reflect on the most memorable gifts you have received. Why can you access those memories so easily? We often attach more meaning to the experience and thoughtfulness from the gift-giver than the gift itself. When people give us that perfect gift, we know they have paid attention to our needs and preferences. And so we feel loved, valued and seen.

THREE THOUGHTS

GOD: The greatest and most consistent gift-giver is You. As James 1:17 states, "Every good and perfect gift is from above."

PARTNER: Which meaningful gifts can I give to my partner with more frequency that help him or her feel loved, valued and important?

ME: I am grateful that God offers me the most pertinent inspiration for the timing and purpose of gifts I can give.

Notes:

DAY FIFTY-EIGHT:
HEALTH

The vitality of our minds, hearts, bodies, spirits, emotions and relationships are tangible indicators of a healthy, balanced lifestyle. Are you healthy and on track in these major life areas? Do you regularly monitor and take steps to improve your health?

Perhaps the conversations of diet, exercise and medical issues are topics you would prefer to avoid. Or, sometimes the realities in life, unexpected circumstances or difficult issues just seem to make it impossible to stick with a well-intentioned plan. It seems more common for people to get off track after initiating said plan than to remain consistent month after month. Of course, couples can enjoy many opportunities to feel close as they embark together on a realistic nutrition and exercise plan.

We can feel anything from guilt, shame and failure to the other extreme of feeling fulfilled, victorious and secure. But when we overcome these realistic barriers, we can help boost our self-esteem, energy levels and positive attitudes. Proper motivation and self-talk prompts us from "I should probably" to "I did it!" statements.

Although not always easy to measure, emotional health plays a very important role in our relationship experiences. Practicing awareness, regulation and expression of our surface emotions such as sadness, anxiety, anger or depression can help us manage inevitable times of conflict, pain and distance. Our partner's safe and sensitive response helps us increase our vulnerability potential to engage and express our deepest feelings such as fear, inadequacy, rejection and abandonment.

Thankfully we are not left to rely on our own strength to stay on track and maintain emotional health. When we design and engage a plan that fits God's will, we can access His power and stick with it, even at our lowest points when we feel like quitting. Second Timothy 1:7 confirms God's generosity in sharing His very spirit: "God did not give us a spirit of fear, but of power, of love and self-discipline."

THREE THOUGHTS

GOD: Redirect me to You and Your written Word so that engaging Your power becomes the first step in my healthy lifestyle plan.

PARTNER: How can I encourage healthy living and support my partner in his or her pursuit of balance and self-care activities?

ME: What small step can I take to better care for my whole being knowing that I bring my best self to my relationships when I am in a healthy place?

Notes:

DAY FIFTY-NINE:
HONESTY

Secret-keeping is harmful to relationships. Yet, family secrets are quite common. Many of us have grown up in families where transparency was strongly discouraged. Perhaps parents want to portray that their family has it all together, or they fear exposing their weaknesses to avoid shame.

When we get stuck only sharing what is on the surface, our relationships will also lack depth. Of course, we don't need to announce every issue, struggle or negative thought we experience. But it makes sense why many of us may struggle with transparency in our adult relationships with friends, coworkers, children and spouses.

Have you ever heard someone say: "Can I be honest with you?" or begin their response with: "To be honest…"? Such responses may have us guessing that everything up to that point was dishonest! Those introductory statements indicate that something more real is coming and the receiver should prepare or brace himself. Some people reveal their preferences to be direct or brutally honest and appreciate when others also "tell it like it is."

However, not everyone's communication style and personality will line up with that approach. The quiet, gentle nature of other people may appear passive. Perhaps a middle ground in which both parties seek to be "tactfully transparent" provides an acceptable balance. The relationship dynamic in which one person interprets a direct, straightforward statement as insensitive and uncaring may require regular discussion and compromise. Overall, two people with distinct approaches can agree on the most effective pathway to honesty.

Since dishonesty harms trust—an essential building block in the foundation of relationships—we must strive to make honesty one of our best habits.

THREE THOUGHTS

GOD: One of the greatest aspects of Your character is Your unrelenting faithfulness to Your promises. Help me to emulate love through truth.

PARTNER: What does my partner need from me in order to be more open and honest? Am I safe, or do I appear or sound judgmental?

ME: In which areas of my life have I been less than honest, and which steps can I take toward transparency?

Notes:

DAY SIXTY:
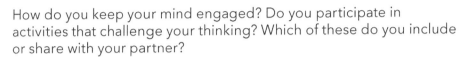
INTELLECTUAL

How do you keep your mind engaged? Do you participate in activities that challenge your thinking? Which of these do you include or share with your partner?

In our romantic and marriage relationships, we can encourage each other to maintain a sharp mind. We grow through adversity as we remain open to different ideas and perspectives. As a couple, we are in a wonderful position to stand behind the desires God has placed in our partner's heart! Engaging the opportunity to support and encourage each other's intellectual interests can produce a sense of individual peace and couple closeness.

When our thoughts are aligned, we naturally feel close. After a while, couples begin to speak in shorthand and can make more accurate guesses as to what the other person is thinking and feeling. Continuing to learn new things and inviting each other into such growth helps them strengthen their sense of intimacy. We can also regularly encourage and strengthen each other's faith. Since faith creates a genuine hope in which we can trust, our minds can rest and find freedom from stress and worry.

Expanding our minds allows us to guide, encourage and impact others. Luke 2 recounts the story of Jesus' boyhood and his hunger for intellectual and spiritual growth—even as a young boy: "Jesus kept increasing in wisdom and stature, and in favor with God and men" (v. 52). Since the capacity for learning never stops, we can commit to being a student for life to learn about many things, including God's wisdom and our partner's heart. To do so, we must hold fast to a humble, teachable spirit.

THREE THOUGHTS

GOD: As Jesus exemplified, I can also remain hungry to learn and pursue wisdom regularly from You.

PARTNER: In which ways and topics can I empower my partner to pursue and share intellectual growth?

ME: I will continue to seek regular opportunities to sharpen my mind and invite my partner to connect intellectually.

Notes:

DAY SIXTY-ONE:
INTERDEPENDENCE

We should pause and ask ourselves the question: "Why did I get into a relationship?" People initiate and remain in relationships for a reason. They see value. A fair balance of give-and-take is expected. And we can quickly begin thinking of our way out of this emotionally-powered entity when we aren't getting our end of the deal.

A popular reason we may seek and stay in a relationship is to feel a strong connection with one other person. We want to matter. We desire to be known and not feel alone.

Choosing to engage someone in a relationship indicates that we would rather be with this person than to not. As a romantic relationship moves toward a stated or felt commitment, the stakes increase. If a relationship advances into a marriage covenant, we must work harder than ever to hold accurate expectations.

Our marriage bond will be challenged as long as we apply the world's way of thinking, "What's in it for me?" and "I deserve…." We forget that marriage is a sacrifice. Have you ever heard a couple at the wedding altar humbly confess: "I can't wait to give up some of my needs and submit to you, to get uncomfortable, to deny my preferences and serve you all the days of my life"? I haven't either.

We think about all the great reasons that we get married, including how this other imperfect person will perpetuate feelings of love, safety and connection. But we forget that we are handing over some of our comforts and control to someone else. Most important, we forget that it's not all about us. Right, this is a very unpopular message.

As explained in Genesis 2:24, God's desire for married couples is oneness: "That is why a man leaves his father and mother and is united to his wife, and they become one flesh."

Whereas *independence* includes living primarily for ourselves, *codependence* involves enabling unhealthy behaviors and patterns and *dependence* represents an unequal distribution of power and investment, *interdependence* requires offering the best parts of ourselves to each other. When two healthy people come together, they have a much better chance of creating a healthy relationship.

Being healthy relationally is often skill-based. Insights are very important, but they need to be practiced and mastered as best as they can be. Each partner can get more "healthy" by learning communication skills as well as understanding, validating and repairing emotional pain.

THREE THOUGHTS

GOD: Help me to understand and meditate on Your purpose and prescription for marriage.

PARTNER: In which three areas does my partner complement me well?

ME: Do I seek and practice a good balance of giving and taking, receiving and serving?

Notes:

DAY SIXTY-TWO:
LOVE

How important is love? Can we give love if we have not received it?

If not from another human, we have certainly experienced love from our Creator! The Bible exalts love to the highest human priority. When asked about the greatest commandment, Jesus declared:

> 'Love the Lord your God with all your heart and with all your soul and with all your mind.' This is the first and greatest commandment. And the second is like it: 'Love your neighbor as yourself.' All the Law and the Prophets hang on these two commandments.

Matthew 22:37-40

Clearly we are instructed to love God with everything in us. He knows that staying connected to the Source of love is what his people most desperately need. Perhaps less clear is the question: "Who is our neighbor?" Of course, neighbors extend far beyond the people living in our neighborhood. Our neighbor is anyone with whom we interact. Most important, our neighbors include those people God has placed right in our homes!

So, how do we practically love someone? Being present is loving. Giving of our time is loving. Listening is loving. And sacrifice is the ultimate expression of love. Love ranges from denying our own preferences, to honoring our partners to help them feel more comfortable, all the way to putting our lives on the line for others. Check with your partner to learn if adding these actions to his or her love preference list will help.

Does your partner need to hear the words? We may feel and express love through various actions but rarely say, "I love you." Again, the most important ways to learn about how to love your partner is to learn from Jesus' teachings and how he modeled love and by asking your partner for the perfect prescription of how he or she feels loved.

THREE THOUGHTS

GOD: More than following a commandment or rule, I will love others for the purpose of bringing glory to You and living my best life.

PARTNER: How would my closest neighbor recognize that I am more generously expressing love through words and actions?

ME: What are the ways in which I feel loved? I will provide examples to my partner of how and when I feel loved.

Notes:

DAY SIXTY-THREE:
NEEDS

We all have legitimate needs. We also have limits. Have you ever asked yourself, "Which needs of mine is my partner designed to meet and is capability of meeting?" No matter how special, insightful and relationally gifted, another human cannot meet all our needs. Our partner can certainly be sensitive and seek to help us feel secure, but this person is not the sole responsible party for our individual sense of emotional security.

In our culture we can view someone with many needs as "needy." You probably don't want to come across as "needy" and recognize that most healthy relationships are reciprocal. Maybe you've had someone in your life that always seemed to take from you in unfair proportions. You may have felt drained emotionally, mentally and physically in such intensive interactions. In some situations, we may need to set limits or boundaries, especially if we start to build resentment. So, when it comes to our romantic relationship, we desire a fair balance in getting our needs met and meeting our partner's needs. But our motivation must be right.

Giving in order to get reveals a contract-view of relationships rather than a long-term covenant vision in which daily balances don't always align. In any given moment, our partner may have a need that is more pronounced than ours. Truly, one of the most difficult moments is when our partner and us both have a strong need for validation at the same time. Each person is expecting the other to relieve, refresh and reset them. But who makes the first move?

The more insight into our patterns and underlying feelings, and the more humble and vulnerable we can become, the greater our capacity for communicating our needs and longings. We must remain respectfully assertive as we express feelings and request specific attention or change in behavior from our partner. For example, we might say, "When you interrupt me, I feel dismissed and invalidated, and I need you to please let me finish my sentence, look at me and hear me."

Our partner can provide an effective source of fuel to lift us up and give us the energy and hope to move forward. But, during parched and disconnected times, we must remember that God is our greatest fuel source and holds an overflowing well of life and hope that never runs dry!

THREE THOUGHTS

GOD: Expose my emotional insecurities and relationship blind spots, and help me to first interact with You so I may strengthen these areas.

PARTNER: Which needs has my partner expressed to me that I can work toward meeting?

ME: How can I communicate a request with respectful assertiveness that my legitimate needs be met?

Notes:

DAY SIXTY-FOUR:
OUTREACH

Stepping out of our realities and into the those of others can create powerful, meaningful and lasting change. Do you recognize and seek to help people who struggle to receive life's basic needs? With guilt and any feelings of condemnation aside, how do you align your blessings with your opportunities to reach out to and lift up those in your community?

Clearly, some of life's seasons are more financially fruitful and thus perceived as more comfortable than others. We can easily get stuck in thinking, "Now is not a good time," but if we wait for a comfortable surplus, most of us may never live to see the perfect time to give. But when we allocate a percentage of our income to giving, we will always have enough to give. Giving out of the overflow and prompting of God versus the pressured motives of man will help us give quietly and for the right reasons.

We model love in action and leave a powerful legacy to impact generations when we give of our time, energy and money. The direct impact of giving selflessly may help offset the entitled feelings in our "I deserve" statements that are so pervasive in our culture. We hold the power to transform the mindset that we do not exist simply to serve ourselves and make our own lives more comfortable. And we enjoy the extra benefit of feeling close to our partner and others as we express this counter-cultural love.

Jesus' eternal mindset speaks about the benefit of serving those in need. Luke 14:12-14 recounts such wisdom:

> *Then Jesus said to his host, 'When you give a luncheon or dinner, do not invite your friends, your brothers or sisters, your relatives, or your rich neighbors; if you do, they may invite you back and so you will be repaid. But when you*

give a banquet, invite the poor, the crippled, the lame, the blind, and you will be blessed. Although they cannot repay you, you will be repaid at the resurrection of the righteous.'

God knows the exponential blessings involved in serving and giving to those in need!

THREE THOUGHTS

GOD: Thank You for sharing the best inheritance! I serve and bless you as I help others. (Read Matthew 25:34-40.)

PARTNER: Tell your partner about your positive feelings when you see his or her heart activated and giving to others.

ME: Which areas can my spouse and I strengthen in terms of giving, helping and serving others outside our home?

Notes:

DAY SIXTY-FIVE:
OVERCOMING

Overwhelming stress and traumatic events hold the power to divide or unite us. In these key moments, it is vital to give and request from our partner the specific love, care and support needed to overcome.

People can be uniquely affected by the same traumatic event because of their distinct experiences and attached meanings. And so, attuning to our partner's subjective grief reaction is essential to remain present and provide specific and timely support. Projecting our own grief timeline can have us feeling impatient and in danger of sending the message to "get over it." We must recognize that our partner may move at a different pace and may process an event very differently than we might.

Grieving is a process, not a one-time event. It may take days or decades to feel fully settled about significant losses, and we must remain aware and sensitive to anniversaries of losses. Both minor reminders and flooding memories can trigger our grief response. So, we need help from God and our partner to access joy and hope amidst our mourning. Ironically, we may turn away from and blame God when calamity strikes. Some tragic events just don't make sense to us. However, people are also more open to an encounter with God when our hopelessness calls for something much greater than our human understanding and coping capabilities.

We can be assured, that no matter what, God is still there! The Apostle Paul exclaims this powerful truth:

> *Who shall separate us from the love of Christ? Shall trouble or hardship or persecution or famine or nakedness or danger or sword? No, in all these things we are more than conquerors through him who loved us.*

> *Romans 8:35,37*

Again, God is always there. He never stops loving us! We can engage God's presence at any time to move from pain, fear, doubt and hopelessness to a real sense of joy, peace and hopefulness!

THREE THOUGHTS

GOD: Thank You for Your awesome presence and eternal faithfulness! Your Spirit and powerful Word makes clear to me that You will always be near.

PARTNER: I will tune in to my partner's emotions and needs surrounding small and big losses and remain aware and sensitive to important dates.

ME: I will consider ways in which we can move from overwhelming to celebrating how we have overcome significant losses.

Notes:

DAY SIXTY-SIX:
PHYSICAL

Feeling physically close includes many more activities than sexual contact. Since physical intimacy is not a synonym for sex, we have countless options to experience closeness. So, if we have shared space, engaged in any physical movement, we can no longer say, "We haven't been *physical* lately."

Movement through an exercise routine at home or in a class provides opportunities to feel close and happy while staying fit. Couples may feel close when they feel supported in their individual fitness routine or as they exercise together. Making sure this time stays fun and encouraging rather than become serious and competitive, couples can enjoy a variety of fitness activities. Whether walking, hiking, jogging, swimming, cycling, lifting weights or taking an exercise class together, the shared sense of movement while maintaining physical health can keep a couple connected on a regular basis.

Dancing can also be a very physically intimate exercise. What better movement is there (with clothes on) that helps you feel close? And it is hard to feel angry or sad when you're following the sweet sound of music and flowing through the air while in each other's arms!

THREE THOUGHTS

GOD: Thank You for giving me my life partner and so many options to feel close!

PARTNER: I will be aware of and ask my partner the three most important ways he or she feels physically close to me.

ME: I will consider and suggest new non-sexual activities that may help us feel closer together.

Notes:

DAY SIXTY-SEVEN:
PROJECT

Do you feel more excitement and connection or frustration and annoyance when working together?

With whatever we do, our sense of connection is on the line. We create memories, whether good or bad, with any significant experience. We may need to think that it's not about how quickly we can finish a project but the journey toward completion. Will we consider how to make the best of this joint project and reach the ideal outcome of feeling close and creating good memories to look back on? Or, will we jump to the thought, "I can do it better myself" and push our partner away, thus create negative memories.

Perhaps some self-talk can help increase our patience when engaging in a project together: "My way is not the only way. My timeline is not the only timeline." Our greatest sense of teamwork results from becoming flexible and remaining open to hearing other methods of visioning and completing a project.

At our local home improvement stores, we might see couples exhibiting a contradicting combination of excitement and frustration. We may also feel these opposing sentiments ourselves. However, two people that feel heard and know that their opinion is valued can create a very positive experience. Cooperating and yielding to different ideas and approaches results in a sense of unity, which naturally ignites intimacy.

A couple working together on any project can enjoy a shared sense of satisfaction when they practice respectful interactions and remeber to enjoy the process.

THREE THOUGHTS

GOD: You are so patient with me. Help me draw on Your perfect character traits to slow down and be gracious with my partner.

PARTNER: Would my partner feel more valued if I invited his or her perspective on a problem or project more often?

ME: I will be more mindful of creating good memories as I view projects as journeys with intimacy opportunities.

Notes:

DAY SIXTY-EIGHT:
RECREATION

When you hear the word "recreation," do you think vacation? What do you do for entertainment? Do you engage in recreational activities often enough?

It is easy to think of fun, easy and relaxing times. Recreation is certainly a diversion from the grind. When busy in their routine, fulfilling responsibilities and feeling tight on time, couples can easily miss out on the fun parts of life. Couples can feel very connected as they escape to a vacation destination. Getting away from our environments for a while can refresh and relax us.

However, more time together does not always translate to an enjoyable time. If in a stressed, tense or conflicted state when embarking on a vacation, a couple can quickly bring their issues to the surface. As much as we'd like to lose this baggage, our problems are portable. They are flexible through times zones and don't need a passport. In these times, we must discuss expectations and anticipate our partner's feelings and responses.

To enjoy these much-needed breaks, our relational skills must also be top-notch. The chances for mutual enjoyment sharply increase when both partners feel heard about ideas and perceive a fair balance of their preferred activities. Our goal is to create great recreational memories rather than thinking or saying, "You ruined this trip!"

So, is all the work worth it? Ecclesiastes 2:22-25 answered this common question:

> *What do people get for all the toil and anxious striving with which they labor under the sun? All their days their work is grief and pain; even at night their minds do not*

rest. This too is meaningless. A person can do nothing better than to eat and drink and find satisfaction in their own toil. This too, I see, is from the hand of God, for without him, who can eat or find enjoyment?

Known to be the richest man who ever lived, King Solomon discovered that without God, our potential for enjoyment is extremely limited. We must regularly create time in our calendars to enjoy an emotionally, mentally, physically and spiritually balanced life. It is when we are healthy and balanced in these areas that we can be most present and active in our most important relationships.

THREE THOUGHTS

GOD: I need You first and foremost. When my purposes and ideas for fun align with Yours, I can experience the greatest fulfillment in my work.

PARTNER: Which recreational activities does my partner like that I can make plans for and add to our calendar?

ME: I will do my part to initiate conversations to help us have proper expectations about and during our times of recreation.

Notes:

DAY SIXTY-NINE:
RESPECT

Does respect have to be earned? Can it be lost?

We learned growing up that being kind to people and being obedient is being respectful. We were told to "respect your elders" and others in a higher position. We may wonder, "Is this person respectable?" In a sense we are lending them respect or extending credit because when we feel mistreated or respect is aggressively demanded, we may lose respect. Similar to parenting approaches, leadership styles can prompt people to do the opposite. Some people will say you start at zero and need to build trust through behaviors. Others may allow you to start at one-hundred percent but deduct points along the way.

In the American culture, listening and giving people eye contact and full attention when they're talking is respectful. We might say, "I can respect that" when we align our values or opinions or agree with somebody. Of course, we can experience difficulty when we see things very differently and when our values or beliefs do not align.

If we feel like we are losing respect for our partner, we can *loan* respect until he or she consistently demonstrates behaviors that helps it grow back. Sharing when we feel a loss of respect during an interaction can help our partner recognize and avoid future, similar words and actions. Most importantly, we must identify what breaks down respect and engage in regular conversations to gain clarity about how to rebuild it.

THREE THOUGHTS

GOD: As I serve and respect my partner today, I will read Matthew 7:12 and the surrounding context: "Do to others what you wish them to do to you."

PARTNER: Knowing what helps my partner feel respected, how can I make sure to demonstrate respectful behaviors and avoid disrespectful ones?

ME: What words and actions must I change to be more honorable and respectable?

Notes:

DAY SEVENTY:
RESTING

How do you know when it's time to unplug? When we feel so rushed that we don't have time to refuel our vehicle, it's a problem!

On those occasions, we more easily recognize the need to slow down. But, of course, our minds and bodies also need regular rest and fresh fuel to continue working as designed. Sometimes we may think we need more caffeine or sugar. Increased amounts may temporarily give us a boost, but what our body really needs is rest. What is your go-to?

Resting to you may be simple. You know you are resting when your eyes are closed and you're asleep. Maybe you take naps and try to enjoy some silence. Many options exist. Other times, doing nothing together is the best way to shut down our minds.

Which relaxing activities do you share? Downtime as a couple may include sitting or lying down in silence, enjoying some light conversation or listening to relaxing music. Or, it may involve slowing down the pace and focusing on caring for each other's bodies. Exchanging foot massages or back rubs, soaking in the tub or showering together can be great practices to keep your marriage fresh!

Creating some relaxing space together can also help. Indoors, you can designate a sitting area in which you only have light conversations, avoiding the tough topics. You can buy a couples sleeping bag and take a daytime nap together. If you have children, you might nap when they do. Outdoors, you can enjoy time together sitting on a porch or deck, or get closer on a swing or hammock.

In whatever ways you choose to relax as an individual and couple, remaining aware of your need to rest and scheduling it on your calendars is essential.

God encourages our rest in Psalm 23:1-3 using peaceful imagery:

> *The Lord is my shepherd, I lack nothing. He makes me lie down in green pastures, he leads me beside quiet waters, he refreshes my soul. He guides me along the right paths for his name's sake.*

THREE THOUGHTS

GOD: I will read and meditate on each verse of Psalm 23 as I thank You for breath and life today.

PARTNER: Does my partner need more space and downtime to rest and recharge?

ME: How can I slow down, create space in my calendar and make time for regular rest?

Notes:

DAY SEVENTY-ONE:
SAFETY

Do you see God as safe and approachable? Sometimes our view of God can parallel our experience with—and feelings about—our earthly fathers. We might have heard that He is distant and doesn't care about our feelings or day-to-day life. But our God is very relational and very approachable!

God is *not* safe if we define safety as expecting Him to give us an easy, predictable and comfortable life. We *will* be challenged in this life. God desires us to grow, and we don't grow by staying complacent. Following His will for our lives means not staying where we are. If we agree that He has the best path for us, we must deny our comforts—and every worldly thing in which we have sought safety—and align ourselves with Him. This step of obedience is the best decision we can make!

So, God may not be safe in our limited view of security, But He *will always* be there and He *will always* care!

Matthew 7:24-25 illustrates how God has our back:

> *Therefore everyone who hears these words of mine and puts them into practice is like a wise man who built his house on the rock. The rain came down, the streams rose, and the winds blew and beat against that house; yet it did not fall, because it had its foundation on the rock.*

Long before Jesus walked the earth, Zephaniah 3:17 declared this secure promise:

> *The LORD your God is with you, the Mighty Warrior who saves. He will take great delight in you; in his love he will no longer rebuke you, but will rejoice over you with singing.*

Lastly, we read in Psalm 46:1-3 of eternal security:

> *God is our refuge and strength, an ever-present help in*
> *trouble. Therefore we will not fear, though the earth give*
> *way and the mountains fall into the heart of the sea, though*
> *its waters roar and foam and the mountains quake with*
> *their surging.*

No other person or thing or system can guarantee such present and eternal security!

THREE THOUGHTS

GOD: Thank You for always being there! Help me to find safety in You alone and to remember that You always have my best interests in mind.

PARTNER: What has made it easy for my partner to share with me on a deeper level?

ME: Am I approachable and safe for my partner?

Notes:

DAY SEVENTY-TWO:
SENSITIVITIES

Do you know those areas in which your partner feels a greater sensitivity? How do you manage these moments? Do you tend to avoid or confront these sensitivities? Or, is it all too easy for you and your partner to escalate into a spinning conflict?

In sensitive moments, we hold the power to either strengthen our connection or fuel our conflict cycles. One of the most difficult instances to navigate is when both partners simultaneously feel stuck in a place of pain and longing, do not feel cared for or understood and lack the energy and hope to take the next step. When we also feel triggered and uncertain how to proceed, we must remain respectful and sensitive rather than tiptoe and avoid emotionally charged areas.

We know we have triggered a sensitivity when our partner's emotional reaction appears exaggerated or doesn't seem to fit the situation. Observing a radical shift in body language, tone or other verbal response leaves us scrambling to figure out what just happened! The obvious emotional tension knocks us off balance and confuses our next steps. Instantly, we process our own emotions while trying to understand and repair this overwhelming situation.

It doesn't seem fair that our insensitivity during critical moments can drown out weeks and months of positive intentions and intimate interactions. But, we all attach a higher value and greater meaning to certain words, actions and situations that get our emotional attention. We all carry different emotional experiences as a result of our individual design and life events. Pushing past overwhelming discomfort and uncertainty is difficult. But thankfully, when bathed in compassion, our genuine validation becomes the bridge to connection.

Seeking to understand our partner on a deeper level communicates that he or she matters and is worth our time and effort. Exhibiting compassion while remaining curious about the deeper, unseen emotions helps us validate the gap and close the distance. Inquiring with our partner about his or her exact needs when a sensitivity arises helps direct our efforts to the most effective acts of empathy.

We show sensitivity to others by demonstrating kindness and compassion. Of course, we want this same genuine care and love from our partner! But, sometimes we need to change the ways in which we request that our legitimate needs be met.

THREE THOUGHTS

GOD: I am thankful for my emotions and how I am prompted to protect myself against oncoming pain. Help me to know when and how to ask my partner to be safe and approachable.

PARTNER: Knowing my partner's sensitive spots, which specific actions of tender, loving care can I demonstrate?

ME: I will communicate to my partner the exact sensitivity I need when he or she approaches my raw areas, vulnerabilities and insecurities.

Notes:

DAY SEVENTY-THREE:
SERVING

Do you notice even a minor imbalance in how you and your partner serve each other?

Some people serve others more readily and frequently. Just because of who you are, you may give a lot more than your partner. And so you may start to feel resentment if your partner does not give back. It hurts! So, an open, loving conversation may help. We can make respectful requests that our partner take steps to notice opportunities to serve us.

People who hold customer service or sales positions face regular opportunities to examine motivations and recall job expectations. They must readily access and strengthen their patience while they take steps to care for a frustrated customer. Wherever the setting, some people feel served when they feel cared for.

Jesus' modeled service to his disciples by washing their feet. He said,:

> Now that I, your Lord and Teacher, have washed your feet, you also should wash one another's feet. I have set you an example that you should do as I have done for you. Very truly I tell you, no servant is greater than his master, nor is a messenger greater than the one who sent him. Now that you know these things, you will be blessed if you do them.

> *John 13:14-17*

How does your partner feel served? We must directly ask our partner to learn which things specifically help him or her feel served. In doing so, we open up another direct pathway to his or her heart. It seems easy to get busy and unknowingly form habits that overshadow service to our partner.

Have you become stuck in a routine that drains your energy or competes with your time to serve your partner? Consider which steps you can take to get unstuck from that rut and more generously serve him or her.

THREE THOUGHTS

GOD: God, thank You! We know how to serve because we can access Your power and learn through Jesus' practical examples.

PARTNER: Ask when and how your partner feels close to you as a result of your loving him or her in practical, selfless ways.

ME: I will serve God and my partner with selfless motives, a humble heart and for the purpose of spreading God's amazing love.

Notes:

DAY SEVENTY-FOUR:
SEXUAL

Consider asking yourself these questions: "Where in the sexual domain is my spouse most sensitive? What does he or she need to feel safe? Am I pressuring her to do things she doesn't feel comfortable doing? Am I sensitive to his vulnerable feelings during the act or discussion of sex? Do I listen well for the deeper, hidden emotions apparent in sex?"

Since sex involves two people, we must consider how often sex is solely about our own needs. Certainly, one person may initiate a sexual engagement because it's on his or her mind. But in those times, are we really thinking about the fulfillment of another's needs? In these times, we may need to engage in open conversations about readiness so nobody feels pressured or forced. Sexual consent is not a one-time decision on a couple's wedding day. It must be given every time.

Although this idea may be controversial, we don't have to wait until we are one-hundred percent emotionally connected and physically energized to have sex. The sexual experience can kickstart a strong emotional connection and vice versa. However, to expect our partners to be vulnerable—emotionally or sexually—after mistreating them is ludicrous.

Having sex is one tangible way in which we feel connected. And particularly for men, it seems, sexual intimacy is one strong tangible way to feel connected when the pathway to an emotional connection seems less familiar or attainable. Nonetheless, beyond the traditional "warming up," both emotional and sexual foreplay is foundational for creating a joint sense of safety and respect that can produce an even greater sexual experience!

However, even in a secure and loving relationship, the area of sex can still produce feelings of shame. With the lights on, many of us feel self-conscious about our body image, parts and functions. Feeling insecure, anxious and ashamed, we need safety, love and support more than ever. Way back in Genesis 2:25, we read that "the man and his wife were both naked and were not ashamed." Such peace and freedom may seem like a dream come true for some of us, but nudity was the norm until sin entered the world. Knowing the answer of course, God asked Adam in Genesis 3:11: "Who told you that you were naked?" The decision to trust Satan's manipulative question tainted perhaps the most natural state and Garden of Eden's culturally accepted ways of being. This critical moment of compromise infiltrated us with the overwhelming feelings of shame, vulnerability and fearfulness.

In regard to sex, communication and safety are the most important elements. We must share what feels good, what hurts, what works for us and what doesn't. Healthy communication includes asking, not assuming. As we send clear, simple messages to our partner, we reduce the frustration connected to our unrealistic expectation of mind-reading and increase the potential for an exciting sexual engagement!

THREE THOUGHTS

GOD: Help me navigate and fully enjoy the private, sacred and very vulnerable topic and experience of sexual intimacy.

PARTNER: What does my partner need from me to participate in a safe discussion about his or her sexual thoughts, feelings, needs and preferences?

ME: Reflecting on my sexual satisfaction, what do I appreciate and would like more or less of?

Notes:

DAY SEVENTY-FIVE:
SHARING

Do you feel comfortable sharing with your partner? If not, how do you work toward satisfying your partner's need for intimately knowing you? Or, as someone who easily shares, how do you handle those inevitable times when you desire more information than your partner readily provides?

By nature, a relationship requires a two-way interaction in which both parties perceive a satisfying balance. More than a daily summary or status report, some people appreciate openness and require more details about their partner's thoughts, feelings and experiences. After all, when we share more deeply with our partner than other people, we are letting this highly valued person into our inner sanctuary.

If our partner wants to know us more deeply, we may need to offer more information even when not completely comfortable doing so. Preparing some talking points prior to interactions can help balance a conversation. Some partners may get stuck giving one-word answers or saying, "I don't know" when hearing surprise questions.

Living on the surface can feel very unsatisfying for both men and women. Yet, the path to deeper intimacy is lined with vulnerability. Sharing deeper feelings such as fear, rejection, failure and inadequacy can feel *very* overwhelming. Like physical safety, we learn rapidly to keep ourselves out of harm's way. We don't need to stop long and think about it. Armed with survival insights, we instantly know what carries potential harm, and we take steps to avoid or mitigate it.

Although letting people step onto our sacred soil can be very difficult, if we desire more closeness, we must act. We can think to ourselves, "You can really only know me to the degree I show me." When risking a step of vulnerability, we may need to alert our partner with a preface such as, "Can I share something with you? It is very hard. Can you please be gentle with me?"

THREE THOUGHTS

GOD: You know all things about me. Help me engage with You to gain courage and discern when and how to share deeper emotions.

PARTNER: Can I initiate a conversation with my partner to schedule regular time to share more deeply?

ME: What do I need from my partner to help me share deeper feelings?

Notes:

DAY SEVENTY-SIX:
SOCIAL

Should our partner or spouse be our best friend? Some people answer affirmatively while others recommend against moving our romantic partner into this position. Perhaps the most healthy arrangement is making sure our spouse is our closest friend, but not our *only* friend.

As discussed earlier, friendship qualities are inherent in romantic and marriage relationships. Knowing we are better together, God designed us for relationships. He desires for us to thrive in community with others, including more people than our romantic partner or spouse. He could have created each one of us with a complete set of gifts, strengths, traits and capabilities. But rather than feel the heartache of emptiness and loneliness inherent within self-sufficiency, God wants us to maximize our potential for intimacy by leaning on others. Hebrews 10:24-25 inspires us to enjoy this fulfilling love:

> *And let us consider how we may spur one another on toward love and good deeds, not giving up meeting together, as some are in the habit of doing, but encouraging one another—and all the more as you see the Day approaching.*

This image of a healthy interdependency illustrates how we need to stay connected to God and others to complement and encourage each other.

Nurturing deep relationships with a few close friends helps us share our uniqueness and spread our deepest love. Proverbs 18:24 states that "a man of many companions may come to ruin, but there is a friend who sticks closer than a brother." Deep friendships allow us to pick up where we left off after long periods of time apart.

Many people crave deeper, more meaningful relationships rather than numerous surface friendships. We feel safe and special when we know that a few others really have our back.

Neglecting our most important relationships seems easy to do when we get busy. When living out of balance, we unintentionally communicate that people are not a priority. Thankfully, spending consistent quality time with God, our partner and close family and friends helps preserve our much-needed sense of connection.

THREE THOUGHTS

GOD: Thank You for placing people around me. Help me identify those people with whom I can go deeper and have courage to take the appropriate next steps.

PARTNER: Does my partner need more time with his or her friends? How can I help make that happen?

ME: To remain intimately connected when physically apart, agree on a realistic frequency of sending texts or emails and leaving voicemails and written notes.

Notes:

DAY SEVENTY-SEVEN:
SPIRITUAL

Sharing when we feel close or distant from God is inviting our partner into one of our deepest places.

Our faith and spiritual journey closely coincides with our sense of intimacy in a relationship or our marriage. Spiritual intimacy can be integrated into every day of our lives. Primarily, we must remember that we are on the same team and we are fighting the right enemy! Spiritual forces are constantly at work trying to bring you down if you love and follow Jesus. Satan is working extra hard to break you up. If you have children that you're helping become lovers and followers of God, you are a triple threat. And if you are trying to minister and help people outside of your family, you grab the attention of the Enemy even more so!

So, expect opposition and be prepared, but remember that you are stronger together. With God on your side, you have an offense that nobody in the natural or supernatural can contend with! But, we can't do this alone. We need people around us who care about and love us, and we vitally need to stay connected to God. It is quite empowering to know that we stand on the shoulders of the believing generations before us. People who believed in, followed and interacted with God have prepared the way. Whether you know it or not, people around you are currently bringing your struggles before God. I am praying for you.

No other sense of intimacy can compare to spiritual intimacy! The sense of intimacy we can feel in knowing that our partner has our back when it comes to meeting with God and helping us fight spiritual battles is matchless.

Even when our marriage is in a tough place, when we feel very distant and don't have much hope that it will improve, we must cling to God's promises. First John 5:14 testifies: "This is the confidence we have in approaching God: that if we ask anything according to his will, he hears us." Although we don't always see immediate change,

He designed our marriage to be the most intimate union right after our relationship with him, and so He is our greatest cheerleader! Knowing that we don't have all the answers helps us remain humble, dependent on and close to God. When we let our spouse into this vulnerable space, we expand our capacity for intimacy.

The legacy of faith and love is more important than anything else. And it all starts with a personal relationship with God.

THREE THOUGHTS

GOD: You promised me: "I am the vine; you are the branches. If you remain in Me and I in you, you will bear much fruit; apart from Me you can do nothing" (John 15:5).

PARTNER: What does my partner need to feel spiritually close with me?

ME: I will engage God's power to grow in faith and hope and view my partner as my teammate during both difficult and exciting times.

Notes:

DAY SEVENTY-EIGHT:
TRUST

Perhaps nothing can hit us harder than a betrayal of trust. We are knocked off balance with little energy left to make sense of the gut-wrenching pain. Someone we thought would be careful with our heart just overwhelmed us with shocking pain. Not feeling like we can naturally go to this person to heal, our devastating blow is magnified by feeling alone.

Trust is closely related to safety. As our sense of security in predictability increases, we begin to feel more settled and able to trust. That's why building trust is a process that includes much more than ticks of a clock. The intangible perception of another human is not easily predictable. Yet, genuine remorse paired with consistent, tangible behaviors can rebuild trust.

Time can help, but time alone doesn't heal. We need to see the offender's repentant heart in action and see, know and feel that something has changed. Whether directly related or not, a new offense may also reset the trust clock. And it is likely that the trust-restoring process will be extended if the betrayed partner discovers the deceit. On the other hand, trust may be renewed sooner if the offender first recognizes, admits and seeks to repair the offense.

So, are *you* trustworthy? How do you know when you have harmed your partner's trust? Even the most adamantly repentant person needs lead time. As the offender, we need to be trustworthy much longer than the offended party's belief that it is real. So, adjusting our expectations to ward off frustrations in our timing disparity is essential. We need to become a safe person in the eyes of our partner once again. Having violated our partner's trust, we must be patient with the subjective process and distinct timelines. Our partner can experience incredible fear at the thought of becoming vulnerable again. After all, we let this person down and have shaken our relationship foundation.

Transparency with consistency can build intimacy. To rebuild trust, the offender must be open, genuine and consistent while the offended partner may need to exhibit grace in the gap of distrust.

THREE THOUGHTS

GOD: When I trust in You first, I gain genuine hope that my partner will remain trustworthy and can give grace and communicate clearly when trust has been harmed.

PARTNER: I must remain aware of the specific words and actions that may harm my partner's trust but will also rebuild it.

ME: What steps can I take to create safety and reassure my partner after my big or small offenses?

Notes:

DAY SEVENTY-NINE:
VALUES

Do you find it easy to elevate the feelings and needs of your most important person? When considering our values, we must also draw attention to our priorities. Our partner will feel valued when we give him or her adequate time and attention.

Over the past few decades, people have become more aware of their need to balance work and home life. Corporate leaders have likely noticed the old-as-time reality that people can perform better when their home life is healthy. Clearly, activities that build self-care and strengthen relationships help us remain grounded and feel a sense of purpose. So, how we choose to spend our time while in a relationship demonstrates what we value in life.

Of course, changes in how we spend our time may shift suddenly or happen gradually. Advancing in our careers or becoming medically ill require adjustment and call our values into action. As we grow older and evaluate priorities, our attention shifts to what really matters in this life. We experience intimacy as we make a difference in the lives of others by loving and serving them. As Matthew 6:21 states, "For where your treasure is, there your heart will be also." Our core beliefs and shifting priorities continue to inform how we express our values and create a worthy legacy.

Assigning our marriage relationship to the highest priority behind God involves feeding our love through regular enrichment. Regardless of our responsibilities, each day we have a choice to create the conditions in which our partner can feel important. Checking out from the world and giving each other our full attention during intimate moments help us believe that nothing else matters. Today becomes tomorrow really fast. We must work at making our todays count before they slip away and become weeks, month and years.

Consider this daily life perspective: "How will I fit everything else in my day after I first make plans that exalt my most important relationships?"

THREE THOUGHTS

GOD: Thank You for designing me with hunger to worship. Help me exalt You to the highest priority so I may fully enjoy all the blessings You have given me.

PARTNER: What helps my partner feel like he or she really matters to me and is one of my highest priorities?

ME: Reflecting on what matters most in life, do I need to realign how I manage my time, money and energy?

Notes:

DAY EIGHTY:
VISIONING

Where is your relationship headed? Who is leading? Are you a faithful follower who holds unswerving confidence in your partner?

Just crossing the finish line at major anniversary checkpoints is not enough. In the long-term, we want to feel the matchless satisfaction in knowing that we hung on, persevered through tough times, felt close and had fun! But we must make this happen. Our future is happening with every second that passes. Do you want a say in how your life unfolds? As a couple, consider asking yourselves: "Knowing who we are and what we value, how do we envision this next love-filled season?"

Creating a joint vision in their relationship, couples can start over, get a re-do and move in an entirely new direction! In the least, they can make a course correction if they have slipped off track. They can recall and re-create activities they enjoyed in the past, but their foundational beliefs and core values must also come along for this wild new ride. Defining roles and responsibilities can put people in charge of different steering and monitoring systems as a couple takes steps to fulfill their mission.

What will you do if your marriage takes a radical, unplanned direction? Our vows keep us strong during storms, but we must secure helpers and acquire and maintain the proper equipment. A sailboat requires numerous important components to keep it sailing. The sails, rudder and steering wheel help us move toward our desired direction. Without wind and water, however, our sailboat is nothing more than a static object. We need to secure and keep God as the captain of our marriage and trust in His leading.

Moreover, we need the help of others. Proverbs 15:22 asserts: "Plans fail for lack of counsel, but with many advisers they succeed." Don't do it alone. Speak with couples that inspire you.

Consult with a marriage counselor or someone in another marriage ministry. Don't just get by and expect that your most important relationships will just happen. Aspire toward the highest level of intimacy!

We all start new every morning with opportunities to shape our sense of intimacy. So, what will you do today?

THREE THOUGHTS

GOD: I trust in Your plans for me and my relationship. Guide us toward the exact places and people that will help us fulfill our calling as a couple.

PARTNER: What does my partner need from me to feel heard and supported as we draft our core vision?

ME: I will pray before considering our new vision and while executing plans. And I will remain open and flexible to God's rerouting.

CONTINUE MAKING INTIMACY HAPPEN!

Notes:

WHERE TO GO FROM HERE

Buy and read through the *40 Forms of Intimacy: Integrating Daily Connection Into Your Couple Relationship* book that contains numerous insights and daily exercises to continue going deeper.

Attend an overview webinar or complete *40 Forms of Intimacy Relationship Series Webinar*, including notes and slides to learn how to go even deeper with your partner.

40 Forms of Intimacy® Workshops & Counseling Intensives

Engage in a live, interactive workshop as an individual or couple with the author! Visit beautiful Colorado for regular workshop opportunities, schedule a private workshop, or find a workshop near you at www.40formsofintimacy.com.

Join us for one-day workshops, and two-day and three-day marriage retreats in Colorado, Mexico, Hawaii and other destinations.

We can also bring *40 Forms of Intimacy®* One-Day Workshops for Couples & Individuals to your location.

Workshops and Counseling Intensives with the Author.

Additional couple enrichment options are available through a variety of workshops in Denver, Colorado. Launching your couple intimacy experience through private counseling sessions could also give you a powerful intimacy boost.

Visit www.relationshipinstitute.org to see a full list of class descriptions that help individuals, couples and families learn how to strengthen their most important relationships.

40 Forms of Intimacy® Small Groups

Participate in a small group with a few other couples to discuss what is working in your relationship and learn many more ideas to increase intimacy.

Connect on Social Media

Enjoy regular relationship inspiration and interaction to keep your intimacy alive!

Facebook: /40formsofintimacybook

Twitter: @40formsintimacy

On the Integrating Intimacy™ Blog at www.40formsofintimacy.com, read new information and interact with other people interested in enhancing their relationship!

Purchase the book at Amazon.com in paperback or Kindle versions!

40 FORMS OF
INTIMACY

Integrating Daily Connection Into
Your Couple Relationship

ALEX A. AVILA

Made in the USA
Coppell, TX
05 December 2020